ONE GAMBLER
TO ANOTHER

RECOVERY *is*
POSSIBLE

**21 Days of Teachings, Affirmations, Activities & Journaling
TO HELP YOU QUIT GAMBLING & FEEL GOOD ABOUT IT**

Cindy Trinidad

#cindytrinidadbooks

My name is

----

and I am a Person in Recovery.

Introduction

I was gambling years before I was old enough to legally place the bet. Almost every morning, for as far back as I can remember, my Father would ask about my dreams. He would interpret them and then bet the numbers that he felt corresponded.

In my country, Trinidad & Tobago, there are State-run games that are drawn four times each day, excluding Sundays and Religious holidays. Father's favorite was called Play-Whe. The game consists of 36 balls which all have a number and symbol written on them. One ball is randomly selected at each draw, offering a payout of $24 for each dollar bet on the winning number.

On the morning of my 16th birthday I had a dream about a large, skinless dog. It stood in a corner while blood dripped from its exposed flesh. When he heard the dream, Father's smile grew big. There was no need to interpret this one. Ball #20 in the game carried the symbol 'Dog' so that was the mark he put all of his money on. Instead of giving me a birthday present he gave me $20 and told me to place a bet for myself.

Although it's illegal for minors to gamble, the neighborhood merchants never refused a bet as long as a child said "My daddy sent me to ..." I placed the entire $20 on the number 20 and won $480 that day. It felt like the best birthday present ever. More than that, it made me believe that I was gifted and could turn my dreams into money.

Father bet the Play-Whe game four times a day, in addition to the Whe-Whe, which was the illegal version run in the community. He never missed an opportunity to play the Lotto and always believed that someday it would make him a millionaire. He kept records of all the numbers that played and spent a great deal of time meditating on these charts for patterns.

Mother played the games as well and encouraged me to pick numbers for my own tickets. Once I had a dream that I was watching television and the lotto was being drawn. I had a ticket in my hand and all of my numbers were being called, except for the last one which I could not see. I told Mother about this dream and she insisted that we play the numbers I saw. We picked a random number for the one that I could not see in the dream and placed our bet. That night, Mother and I stood in the living room and watched all of our numbers pop up on screen, except for the last one which I didn't see in the dream.

We fell short of the million dollar jackpot but won some money which we never mentioned to Father. If a number was drawn and we had a feeling it would play but did not place a bet, Father would fly into a rage. Mother and I knew that he would not have been happy for our lotto jackpot-miss. More than likely, he would have said that we didn't try hard enough to decipher the last number which I didn't see in my dream. He would not be grateful for the money we won but would instead pressure me to dream better, as if it was something I could control.

Gambling was so normal in our home, that I didn't know it carried a stigma until I was in my late 20s.

At age 26 I became a single mom. My baby was born with a hole in her heart and when the doctors revealed this to us, my partner hopped on a plane to New York. He threw away our 10-year relationship and left me to fend for myself.

I couldn't work because of the amount of time I had to stay in the hospital with my baby, so for about a year, I lived off my savings. When that was depleted, I used my credit card. When that was maxed out, I sold every valuable thing that I owned, including my bed. My last resort was social welfare.

I was down to my last $10 one day and needed diapers for my baby. At that point I'd taught myself Poker and was good at it. I believed my gambling skills could turn that $10 crumb into a feast, so I went to a nearby casino and spent a few hours playing a video poker machine. In the end, I walked away with $3,000.

In the years that followed, I was able to build back my life financially while my daughter's heart healed. I held high-paying jobs and started several businesses. As my money grew, so did my tolerance for risks. I switched from Poker to Roulette after a guy I worked with explained that it was "just like Play-Whe" with its 36 numbers. The only difference was the roulette had two extra numbers, 0 and 00.

I immediately fell in love with the Roulette game. The payouts were higher than the Play-Whe, with $36 given for every dollar bet and $90 if the gold powerball was called. Best of all, I didn't have to wait hours for a game. The Roulette supplied a winning number every 60 seconds.

I loved the Roulette but it didn't love me back. It was like being in a bad relationship. I'd give all my time and money but it would only deliver heartbreak. When I was wounded and ready to quit, it would offer a giant win to toy with my emotions and convince me to stay.

I once scheduled a 2-week vacation from work. I kept it a secret because I didn't want anyone trying to monopolize my time. My intention was to pretend that I was going to work but instead spend my days in the casino multiplying the $2500 that I put aside for the occasion. Everything was set in place until Mother asked me to do her a favor.

Some years earlier, she had taken out an insurance policy for my daughter on my name. She was now upset with her agent and wished to cash out the policy valued at $17,700. Because the policy was prepared on my name, I had to be the one to go in and collect the cheque. I now had $20,200 in my hand and 2 weeks of free time.

I lost all of the money in 2 days and had to explain to my Mother what happened. Instead of throwing a fit and spewing vulgarities, she calmly asked, "Do you have anything saved for your child?" The truth is, I wasted thousands of dollars chasing numbers and never once saved a cent for my daughter. Even worse, I gambled away the little inheritance that my mother set aside for her ... and I felt no remorse.

I was dead on the inside. The only thing I ever felt was irritability when I couldn't play Roulette. I got no pleasure from going to the movies, listening to music or even being with my family. The only thing I wanted to do was visit my favorite casino, sit in my chair and bet on numbers.

This particular gambling binge opened my eyes and made me realize that I had a serious problem. A decent human being would have regret and at least offer an apology. But I felt nothing. No guilt. No shame.

That instance where I took $10 and turned it into $3,000 sounds amazing when I tell the story a certain way but the full truth is, I left my 3 month old baby at home, alone and asleep in her crib, while I gambled for hours. That is the risk I took and then justified my behavior because I had a gambling problem and could not see it.

One of my most profitable business ventures was a media production company that specialized in wedding videography and photography. I stopped gambling out of necessity but instead, sunk the majority of this business' profits into the roulette for recreation. I became so fixated on the roulette that I spent the majority of my workday in the casino and turned down jobs. My cash supply ran low but instead of getting back to work, I decided to sell 2 of my cameras to my friend who was a Pastor, for the small sum of money that he could afford to pay. This sum was significantly less than what the cameras were worth but I re-branded it "seed money" which I intended to bet, multiply and use to purchase even better cameras. I lost everything and then accused my Pastor-friend of exploiting me because he knew I had a problem and still facilitated the sale. I refused to be held accountable for my actions.

I used another friend as a safety net for moments when I gambled away my earnings. Once, I told him that I was robbed when I actually lost my money in the casino. This friend was significantly less well-off than me and slept in a corner of his grandmother's kitchen, yet I bled him dry without conscience. He was battling a cocaine addiction and believed that we were suffering the same. I knew that whenever I had no other options, he would always give me his last dollar.

I was a horrible person but I could not see it. I found a way to justify all of my bad behavior and twisted situations to sound interesting, when in fact, I was hurting my loved ones and myself.

Some weeks after the gambling binge with my Mother's insurance money I made a decision to quit. I gave up the State-run games, Roulette and even the games on my phone. The withdrawal symptoms were painful and much like the ones experienced by drug addicts. It was an uphill battle building back the trust of the people I'd hurt but choosing to live gamble-free has 100% been worth it.

Whether you purchased this book yourself or received it from a well-meaning relative or friend, I'm happy that you're reading. I want you to know that Recovery is possible and that you can get back to a state of normalcy.

It is possible to wake up and not immediately think about the game. You can live free from lies, deception and manipulation. You can be free from that constant itch and urge to gamble. Free from the sadness and weight of losing.

You can have a genuinely good life where you don't have to carry the stigma of being a gambling addict. A life where you don't have to count your clean days and feel like a failure when you relapse. You can have a full, meaningful life where you are actually Free.

In this book, I will offer you a pathway.

It is not the only path that can help you to reach your goal, but it is my method and it works. All I ask is that you let go of resistance, open yourself to the teachings and do the exercises. Your success ultimately depends on your participation and commitment to the process. Read slowly and reflect on what is being said. Do not skip ahead. The book is structured for one lesson to be taught each day. There are affirmations for you to say, activities for you to do and journaling spaces for you to write about your urges, thoughts and experiences.

There is no magic or mystery involved.

You must put in the work to receive the benefits.

I gambled for 20+ years. I have been where you are right now and I know how you feel. One gambler to another, I promise you that your life can be turned around for good. There is genuine freedom ahead. Commit to this process for 21 days and see for yourself.

I wish you peace on your journey ...

GAMBLING DISORDER DIAGNOSIS

The Diagnostic and Statistical Manual of Mental Disorders, Fifth Edition (DSM-5) is published by the American Psychiatric Association and is the handbook used by health care professionals around the world as the authoritative guide to the diagnosis of mental disorders.

To meet the criteria for a Gambling Disorder diagnosis, an individual has to have at least four of the problems identified below, within a 12-month period, in addition to persistent and recurrent gambling behavior that leads to clinically significant impairment or distress.

The individual:

- Needs to gamble with increasing amounts of money in order to achieve the desired excitement.

- Is restless or irritable when attempting to cut down or stop gambling.

- Has made repeated unsuccessful efforts to control, cut back, or stop gambling.

- Is often preoccupied with gambling (mentally reliving past gambling experiences, planning their next venture, thinking of ways to get money with which to gamble).

- Often gambles when feeling distressed (e.g., helpless, guilty, anxious, depressed).

- After losing money gambling, often returns another day to get even ("chasing" one's losses).

- Lies to conceal the extent of involvement with gambling.

- Has jeopardized or lost a significant relationship, job or educational / career opportunity because of gambling.

- Relies on others to provide money to relieve desperate financial situations caused by gambling.

Mild: 4–5 criteria met.
Moderate: 6–7 criteria met.
Severe: 8–9 criteria met.

Gambling involves decision making, based on the assessment of risk and reward. You place something of value (money, jewelry) at risk, in the hope of gaining something of greater value.

Forms of gambling include lotteries, card games, animal racing (horse, dog, goat, snail, pigeon), sports betting, casino machines (slots, roulette), internet gaming and to some degree the trading of foreign exchange (forex) and cryptocurrencies.

Your family and friends might look at your behavior and say that you have a gambling problem but an official diagnosis can only come from a qualified practitioner who uses the DSM-5 as their guide. The most important indicator of a problem however, is the way that you feel before, during and after you gamble. Only you will know the extent of your struggles.

Be honest with yourself as you evaluate your situation. Remember that you can receive help for your condition only when you admit that you have a problem. Admit that it is difficult for you to manage, then open yourself to the teachings and put them into practice.

Day 1

AFFIRMATION

**Recovery is Possible
and it is possible for Me.**

My urge to gamble is:

0	1	2	3	4	5	6	7	8	9	10

none   high

I am feeling...

_____

_____

_____

_____

_____

_____

_____

_____

_____

_____

_____

_____

_____

_____

_____

_____

_____

_____

_____

_____

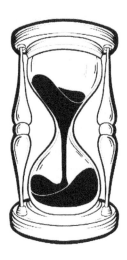

RECOVERY IS POSSIBLE

Today is an important day because you have made the choice to begin the process of healing your life. Realistically, you might have several Day 1's and that's okay. It is normal to want a change, to be passionate about it, to try your best and then relapse. We've all been there. What's important is to focus on doing the best that you can in the moment, and to be gentle with yourself.

There are no secrets to recovery. Everything you need to know to recover from a gambling disorder is available, accessible and quite simple ... You just have to turn your back on all forms of gambling and consciously choose healthier activities every day.

There are no shortcuts to recovery. Recovery is a process and it is as multidimensional as you are. It takes time to heal, to rebuild trust, to mend broken relationships, to get your finances in order and to pay off debts.

The good news is that when you change your mindset, you will change your life. On this journey, you will be invited to change the way you think about yourself, your circumstances and money.

Through a bit of introspection we will get to the root of why you gamble. Once you start pulling out the roots and addressing these core issues, gambling will have less and less reasons to be a part of your daily routine.

Substitution is an essential part of this recovery process.
You will be required to trade gambling for something else … something that is morally and socially acceptable like group meetings, religion, sports, community work or hobbies. Your mind needs to be occupied. Your hands need to be busy. Your time needs to be filled constructively. Persons who try to quit gambling and do not adjust their mindset, do not get to the root of their problem and do not substitute gambling for something healthier, end up being the ones most prone to relapse.

Commit to doing the exercises. Put in the work and trust that it leads to a healthier you at the end of these 21 days. Let go of resistance. Stop shooting down the assistance and advice given by others. **Train your brain to see the ways in which something will work, instead of looking for a reason why it won't.** Look for the yes. Look for the positive.

Adopt the mindset, "How can I make this work for my benefit?"

LOCUS OF CONTROL

You are as strong as your mindset will allow you to be.
You will be successful in proportion to your belief that you can recover from this gambling disorder.

A person who has an External Locus of Control believes that events outside of themselves are responsible for their successes and failures. When they win, it is because of luck or destiny and when they lose, it is always someone else's fault. They believe that they are powerless over situations and never want to be held accountable for their actions.

When you have an Internal Locus of Control, you understand that every action produces a result and because of that, you have the power to create the outcomes you desire. You know that your efforts matter and so, you do not sit around waiting for miracles to happen or for opportunities to land in your path. You are able to accept praise for a job well done and can accept responsibility when things do not turn out right.

Having a strong Internal Locus of Control is a desirable trait. People easily recognize it within you even if they are unfamiliar with the term Locus of Control itself. Employers favor employees with a strong Internal Locus of Control because they know those persons will be more responsible and dependable. In general, a person with a strong Internal Locus of Control does not make excuses and does not nurture a victim mentality. They routinely engage in introspection and have a desire to grow in all areas of their life. They know that a change in their behavior can have a meaningful impact on their future.

I used to blame my Father for introducing me to gambling. I felt exploited because he never gave me an option to say no. He used my dreams to source the numbers that he bet and essentially put the responsibility for his wins and losses on a child. He and my Mother set a poor example for me to follow from a very young age but they never forced me to become a gambler as an adult. I made that choice for myself. Every day I chose to withdraw my money from the bank, visit the casinos in my community and bet until I lost everything. As an adult I was free to choose differently but I didn't. Recovery would not have been possible if I kept blaming my parents for the consequences of my own actions.

Search yourself.
Do you identify with having an External or an Internal Locus of Control?

To increase your Internal Locus of Control you simply have to focus inward and take responsibility for the part you play in situations instead of pointing the finger at others. From here, you focus on solutions because you know that they are available to you.

ACCOUNTABILITY & RECOVERY

You are not a victim.

Nobody forces you to sit in front of a screen for hours and gamble away all of your money. You make the conscious decision to do that. Gambling is not something that just happens to you. It is not a disease like cancer which can still progress in spite of treatment and lead to death. Your problems are created because of your unwillingness to say no to the game. At some point you have to face these truths and be accountable for your actions.

Accountability starts with "I".

A gambler often says, "Gambling is ruining my life."

Accountability says, "I am ruining my life by choosing to gamble."

You are the only one capable of fixing your circumstances.

You have the ability to heal all of the things that are broken but it will not happen by wishing, hoping and feeling sorry for yourself. There has to be a change in behavior, which can only occur when you purposely create a shift in your mindset.

There is no power in the label "addict". It is a negative term that has no positive value. It simply encourages people to scorn and humiliate the ones who carry the label. Gamblers often hide behind the word addiction as a way to avoid accountability and to make it seem like there is no choice involved. The word is used as a crutch to stay in the game, to stay weak and to manipulate others into being sympathetic.

You can admit that you have a problem and receive help without branding yourself for life, and carrying the weight and stigma of the addiction label.

Are you currently working towards a healthy, gamble free life?
Or are you thinking of yourself as an addict and running from the gambling demon?

Whatever you focus on will grow.
If your focus is on your "sickness" then you are not actively making room for wellness. You will remain in bondage if you speak constantly about your struggles to quit and hold on to the false belief that quitting is hard. You will never be free if you keep thinking about your losses and hoping that one last bet could fix your problems.

To be well and free you have to think, speak and act in ways that produce wellness and freedom. It is easier to form new habits than it is to stop doing something altogether. **Instead of "trying to quit", focus on the healthier things that you can do instead of gambling.** Stop running from the bad and hoping that it will leave you alone.
Walk towards what is healthy and good.

Write A Letter To Yourself

Writing at this stage of your recovery can aid in releasing feelings and thoughts that are raw and unfiltered. Write about your pain. Describe the person who you are right now. Describe what freedom from gambling means to you.

_____

_____

_____

_____

_____

_____

_____

_____

_____

_____

_____

_____

_____

_____

_____

_____

_____

_____

_____

Day 2

AFFIRMATION

I am worthy of Redemption.

I am worthy of Love.

I am worthy of Forgiveness.

I am worthy of a Future.

I am worthy of Peace.

My urge to gamble is:

0	1	2	3	4	5	6	7	8	9	10
none										high

I am feeling...

_____

_____

_____

_____

_____

_____

_____

_____

_____

_____

_____

_____

_____

_____

_____

_____

_____

_____

_____

_____

_____

_____

_____

_____

_____

MAKING THE DECISION TO QUIT

The desire to quit always comes after a terrible loss. When you're up and experiencing a streak of good luck, there is seldom the resolution to walk away and put the bets behind you. This begs the question:

Do you genuinely want to stop gambling or do you just hate losing?

Do you pledge to quit because _in that moment_ of losing your money, you realize that gambling has cost you too much? Do you feel guilty _in that moment_ but bounce right back to the game after the guilt has subsided? _Does quitting only cross your mind when you think about your losses or is it something that you have a strong desire to do even when you win?_

For most gamblers, quitting becomes an emotional response, much like the tantrum thrown by a child who doesn't get their way. Quitting that is tied to a loss will not last because it is not grounded in logic. As soon as the negative emotions wear off, the urge to gamble will pop up and you will give in.

Think about the reasons why you want to quit. Go deeper than just saying "It's costing me too much money." Search yourself and figure out if quitting is really what you want.

The desire to quit must come from within you.
No outside pressure or ultimatum from loved ones has the power to truly stop you. No program will be effective until you make that resolute choice to stop for good because you want to stop, for your own good.

Always remember that you have free will.
You have the choice to quit or to continue gambling.
If your family pressures you to stop and you don't, then they can leave. You can always get a new spouse and have more children. You can always gain new friends and even get new jobs. Let's be real here. You will always have access to money and can always find a way to play.

But is the game really worth losing everything that you currently have? Is it worth having to lie, steal or borrow money and incur debts that you have to struggle to repay? Is the game worth all the pain?

You are not obligated to quit gambling.
It is a choice that you have to make and genuinely want, especially when you're on your good days and have money in your hand.

CONTROLLING YOUR GAMBLING

You've invested in your game for years, believing that if you play enough, the Big Win will come. In some ways, you believe that you are owed a Big Win. When you experience a huge loss, you tell yourself that you're done but return to the game shortly thereafter. You exist in a state of conflict where you want to quit but also want to continue playing. You believe that you can control your gambling or at least hope that it is possible to do so.

My friend, when the ship is sinking it is wise to get off. Jump into the life raft and sail away. You don't stay aboard a sinking vessel and hope that it stays afloat. You do what is necessary to preserve your life and you do it quickly.

Refer to the DSM-5 guideline for the diagnosis of a Gambling Disorder. If it describes you, then it's clear you have a problem. You will never be able to balance or manage your gambling. It will always spiral out of control and bring devastation to your life.

It is said that a person has to hit rock bottom before they decide to quit for good. Rock bottom entails losing everything ... your job, money, relationships and even yourself.

Rock bottom is not something to strive for. Rock bottom is not a place of empowerment. Rock bottom is when the game decides it is done with you. It strips you of everything and spits you out. You have no other option but to quit.

Imagine losing everything, including your support system, and trying to rebuild your life from scratch. If you are having a hard time now, imagine how much worse it will be at rock bottom, starting over with nothing.

Recovery is not penance or punishment.
It doesn't take anything away from you. Recovery actually adds to your life and ensures that you have a meaningful one.

Right now you have the skewed perception that gambling can do something positive for you. It makes you happy and gives you free money. But this is an illusion. **Gambling is a business and you are actually purchasing very expensive entertainment. Every time you play, you are making the owners of casinos and betting websites wealthier.**

While you are wishing for a jackpot, they are taking your rent money and savings to purchase luxury vehicles, mansions and designer clothes. They are vacationing in exotic locations while you are staring at a screen and playing their games. You are funding their lavish lifestyle, while stretching your last dollar and hoping for that elusive Big Win.

As long as you keep gambling, their income is sure. As long as you keep showing up, they will never have to worry about paying their bills. Who is the real winner here?

Make a choice today.
Whose life is more important to invest in, yours or theirs?

ACTIVITY - DAY 2
State Your Reasons For Quitting

_____

_____

_____

_____

_____

_____

_____

_____

_____

_____

_____

_____

_____

_____

_____

_____

_____

_____

_____

_____

_____

Day 3

AFFIRMATION

I have the ability to make better choices.

I let go of everything that blocks my Recovery.

I choose to hold on to what is good & healthy.

My urge to gamble is:

0	1	2	3	4	5	6	7	8	9	10
none										high

I am feeling...

_____

_____

_____

_____

_____

_____

_____

_____

_____

_____

_____

_____

_____

_____

_____

_____

_____

_____

_____

_____

_____

SELF EXCLUSION, GAMBAN & GUARDIANSHIP

During my intervention I asked, "How do I stop gambling?"

My Mother quickly responded, "Just stop going!"

In the moment, her answer seemed too simple and empty. I felt like she didn't understand the complexities of what I was struggling with. She didn't understand the urges and the torment, the thrill of the game nor the relationships I formed at the casino. How could I, just stop going?

Years later, I realized that my Mother's simple advice was right. If you're serious about turning your life around and getting this demon off your back, then you have to stop going towards the pain. The fact is, you can only gamble if there is a game and if you have the money to play. You will always have access to money, so the first step forward is to eliminate the game.

Self-Exclusion is a method of quitting whereby you visit your favorite casino and ask to be banned. You will be given forms to fill out and you will supply them with a photograph of yourself / identification. The ban is legal and applies to all participating casinos within the self-exclusion coverage area. If you've chosen to self-exclude and then find yourself at the casino, you can be arrested and charged for trespassing.

Self-Exclusion places the burden on other people to ensure that you do not gamble. In cases where security doesn't catch you at the door and you happen to slip inside, you will not be able to cash in any jackpots that you might win. The casino will still take any money that you have lost.

Self-Exclusion will not apply to regular businesses that have a few gaming machines on the side. It is only available at casinos that choose to participate in the self-exclusion program.

Gamban is a subscription software that blocks access to over 60,000 gambling websites and apps worldwide. It blocks everything that is transactional, including cryptocurrencies and trading websites. It can be installed on up to 15 of your devices. The cost of the service is minimal and you have the option to pay for it with debit and credit cards or through PayPal. You can pay monthly or yearly and there is a free 7-day trial. Gamban works well for persons who are addicted to online gambling. Visit www.gamban.com for this service.

If there is someone in your life that you trust, you can appoint them to act as a Guardian for your money. This person will have sole access to your funds, while you relinquish control. They will hold your debit and credit cards and issue cash based on the budget you set.

Self-Exclusion, Gamban software and Financial Guardianship are secondary measures put in place for moments when your urge to gamble becomes unbearable. They are safety nets.

You hold the primary responsibility for your recovery. The onus is on you to avoid bars, restaurants and any other establishments where temptation lurks.

You have to police yourself.

What secondary measures / safety nets have you put in place to prevent yourself from gambling when the urge pops up?

_____

_____

_____

_____

_____

_____

_____

_____

_____

_____

_____

_____

_____

_____

_____

_____

_____

_____

_____

_____

_____

_____

_____

Join An Online Support Group

There are millions of people around the world who struggle with a gambling disorder. You are not alone in this.

There are many support groups on Facebook where you can share your journey and seek comfort in times of trial.

The one I lead is called One Gambler To Another
www.facebook.com/groups/onegamblertoanother

You can also do a search for Gambler's Anonymous and connect with other people who understand your struggles.

Day 4

AFFIRMATION

I consciously choose NO today.
NO is essential to my healing.

My NO is sure.

I am not going to waste my money.
I am not going to waste my time.

NO!

My urge to gamble is:

0	1	2	3	4	5	6	7	8	9	10
none										high

I am feeling...

_____

_____

_____

_____

_____

_____

_____

_____

_____

_____

_____

_____

_____

_____

_____

_____

_____

_____

_____

_____

_____

_____

RESISTING TEMPTATION

You are never on auto-pilot. Your brain is always working.

When the idea to gamble pops into your head, you tell yourself that you should not play. The urge persists and you then consider the logistics. This is where the problem starts. You plan how to get to the casino or plan which websites to browse. You make a mental budget and decide how much money you can spare. You negotiate with your conscience and rebrand things to make them more acceptable.

You consider money to be capital that you are investing or multiplying. Losses are weighed against the potential of big wins. You are hopeful and believe that the odds will come in your favor. You make peace with risking and even losing the small sum you set aside for this last bet. Once inside the game, more mental activity takes place. Greed sets in and you choose not to cash out. You try to recoup the money you've lost within the past few days or weeks. You invest more and more money, hoping to catch a jackpot, until your account runs dry.

You are in a constant battle with your mind. It is like a wild horse that needs to be bridled and tamed. **Your mind is led astray by misplaced Hope and Faith.** You hope that luck would be on your side. You look for favorable signs and convince yourself that a win is sure to come. Whenever you are tempted to gamble you have to remember that your mind, the wild horse, is chasing an illusion.

Cling to Reality.

The fact is, you will always lose more than you will win.

There are days when you will have a good payout but you will never recover the thousands that were lost. You might win some money but you will lose valuable time with your children, friends and family. Your personality will suffer and you will become dull and irritable. You will lose yourself to a game. You will sit in front of a screen but you are the one being played.

Temptation always resurfaces when the pain of your financial loss wears off. Put measures in place so that it is harder for you to play when temptation arises. Self-Exclude, install Gamban software and appoint a Financial Guardian. Avoid hanging out at places that have gambling facilities. Limit the amount of cash that you carry.

When tempted to gamble, focus on the ways in which gambling hurts you. Think of how low you feel when you lose everything... how it feels when you cannot provide for your children... how ashamed you feel when you have to borrow money.

The games position you to lose significantly more than you will ever win. The casinos are beautiful and lavish because they are making a profit. If gambling was benefiting the players, then business would be bad for the Owners and they would close down. But the casinos are earning billions of dollars because regular people are losing their paychecks and savings.

Your money should be used to improve your life, not gambled away to make casino owners wealthier.

A casino sent a couple of match play coupons in the mail at my Mother's house because I used her address when I signed up for my membership. The coupons were placed in the mail without my name and at that time Mother had no idea that I was a casino gambler. She was confused as to why this prominent member's club sent coupons to her home but she eventually shrugged it off and tucked the coupons in a draw.

Every time I passed that draw it felt like it lit up and I could almost hear the coupons calling my name. At that time, I was on a gambling hiatus. Staring at the bright roulette screen for hours caused me to suffer intense headaches, so I paused gambling for a few months. These coupons became the trigger for my relapse. I ended up waiting a month for Mother to forget about the coupons before I took them and cashed them in. What I should have done was tear them up the day they came.

It seemed like every time I made up my mind to quit, something would pop up to lure me back to the game. The workers at another casino kept calling my phone to tell me about their promotions. No matter how many times I asked them to take me off their call list, they would always promise to do it, but call me anyway. I had to change my phone number to get away from them.

I was watching a stand-up comedy special and halfway through the show, the comedian voiced an ad for an online gambling site. They sponsored his show and he was fulfilling his contractual obligations by introducing them to his audience.

The fact is, you can be innocently browsing the internet or using an app on your phone and some form of gambling advertisement could pop up.

While these things can be triggering and upsetting, you have to be mindful of the fact that casinos and gambling sites are businesses and they have the right to advertise. They have a right to market their services and to seek out new customers just like every other business. They are not obligated to care about you and they do not owe anything to your recovery.

Your recovery is your business.

Focus on yourself and your healing and allow other people to do what benefits them.

Strengthen your NO. Take a cold shower. Call your Sponsor.

STRENGTHEN YOUR NO

Desire is never quenched.
You will experience a temporary moment of satisfaction when you get the thing you want but soon after, a desire will pop up for something else. This is human nature. When it comes to gambling, you will always crave bigger risks, bigger thrills and bigger wins.

In recovery, there is a need for discipline and restraint.
If you are serious about quitting, then you must strengthen your NO.
NO is like a muscle that needs to be worked regularly in order for it to be powerful.

NO is a complete sentence.
It doesn't require a follow up or justification.
When family or friends suggest going to the casino or places where games are available, you owe it to your recovery to say NO.

It is understandable that you want to be social and engage in regular activities like everyone else ... but you are not like everyone else. You belong to the 1% of the population who has a gambling disorder.

When the average person can play for 10 minutes and walk away, you cannot. You are accustomed to playing for hours, draining your savings and wagering your last dollar. Your mindset is different and it is hard for a person without this problem to understand.

When the desire to play pops up
you must issue a firm NO.
Remind yourself that NO is essential
to your healing.

Consciously choose NO.

What are the things that trigger you or tempt you to gamble?
How do you plan to combat these triggers and temptations?

_____

_____

_____

_____

_____

_____

_____

_____

_____

_____

_____

_____

_____

_____

_____

_____

_____

_____

_____

_____

_____

_____

_____

_____

Participate In A Meeting

Attend a Gamblers Anonymous meeting, online or in-person, and actively participate. Introduce yourself to the group and share a bit of your experience.

Day 5

AFFIRMATION

.

I am allowed to be free.

I will answer to a new name.
I am a Person in Recovery.

I will Think, Speak and Act in ways
that produce wellness and freedom.

My urge to gamble is:

0	1	2	3	4	5	6	7	8	9	10
none										high

I am feeling...

_____

_____

_____

_____

_____

_____

_____

_____

_____

_____

_____

_____

_____

_____

_____

_____

_____

_____

_____

_____

_____

_____

MY NAME IS:

ANSWER TO A NEW NAME

Degenerate gambler. Pathetic. Addict. Loser.

These are just some of the labels placed on gamblers. I'm sure you've heard them all and quite a few others as well. Most of the time it's your family and friends who sling these derogatory terms your way when you lose money.

The gambler who wins is praised and admired, while the one who ends up in financial ruin becomes the object of ridicule and scorn. Your words cease to have value. Nobody believes your promises, so when you vocalize your desire to quit, you are greeted with skepticism. Every time you leave the house, your family questions where you're going and where you've been. Once you are branded a compulsive gambler you are no longer trusted by those you love.

People will say hurtful things *to* you and *about* you, but your perception of yourself is what matters above everything else. If you consider yourself a loser, a failure and a reject, then this is who you will ultimately become. This is the essence of the Self-Fulfilling Prophecy, as taught in Psychology. **The way you think about yourself, good or bad, is who you will eventually be.**

If you believe that you are an addict who cannot do anything right, then Life will give you more opportunities to prove this to be true. If you believe that you are powerless and will never be free from throwing away your money behind a bet, then you will remain in bondage.

Freedom from a gambling disorder is possible.
You can be free to the point where the game doesn't cross your mind. Free from the itch and urge to play. You can be free to find pleasure in doing regular things without wagering and depending on luck. **Ultimately, your success and freedom depend heavily on your perception of yourself and the thoughts that you nurture.**

Answer to a new name.
Once committed to quitting and healing, you are no longer a "gambling addict". You are a Person in Recovery; a Person who previously gambled.

CHOOSE HEALTHY SPEECH

Words have the power to hurt and destroy but they also have the power to heal and create. If you keep speaking negative things *to* yourself and *about* yourself, more and more negative things are going to manifest for you.

Practice speaking positively over your life. Look at yourself daily in the mirror and repeat your affirmations. Cling to words of encouragement.

If you shift your mindset to one of hope, possibility and goodness, then negativity should not roll off your tongue. Speak little of your struggles and weaknesses. Your days may be hard and sometimes depressing, but as much as possible, refrain from talking about it constantly and especially to people who cannot provide solutions. Further to this, avoid people who speak more about hardships and woes than they do about goodness, solutions and ease.

Belief is cemented by repeatedly hearing a particular message. As human beings we are inclined to believe the things that we hear, over and over. If you are surrounded by people who speak negatively to you all of the time, at some point you are going to believe their words. One small insult that you hold on to becomes like a seed planted in your brain. In time, it will grow and poison the way you think about yourself.

None of us are 100% immune to criticism. As a gambler, you will receive a heap of negativity from family and friends when your habit depletes savings and creates debts. As much as people believe they have the right to vent, you also have the right to preserve your mental health. Their right to vocalize their pain is not greater than your right to heal.

You are allowed to grow and evolve.
If the people closest to you care about your recovery, then they should be willing to participate in it. If you have made the decision to live gamble-free and you are actively working towards wellness, then it is fair and within your rights to walk away from anyone who continuously puts you down. Let that person know who you are today. This version of yourself does not need a constant reminder of past mistakes.

Choose healthy speech.
Guard your ears. Guard your tongue.

Create A Vision Board

A vision board is a visualization tool that you can create using photos & words. It helps you to identify what matters most to you and helps you to be clear on what you want to achieve. It motivates and enhances productivity.

Create a vision board in the space available here. Collect photos of the things you want and stick them to the page. You can also create a larger version of your vision board to hang in a spot in your home where you can see it every day.

Day 6

AFFIRMATION

I choose to focus on Hope,
Possibility and Goodness.

My urge to gamble is:

0	1	2	3	4	5	6	7	8	9	10
none										high

I am feeling...

_____

_____

_____

_____

_____

_____

_____

_____

_____

_____

_____

_____

_____

_____

_____

_____

_____

_____

_____

_____

_____

MANAGING NEGATIVE EMOTIONS

A few years ago in my country, a man drove his car off a roof-top garage and plummeted 30-feet to the ground after losing $1,300 at a casino. He survived the fall but suffered severe spinal injuries. One moment of overwhelming negative emotions escalated to create a lifetime of irreversible pain.

Losses often feel devastating in the moment.
You might feel angry for wagering so much of your funds. You might feel guilty because that money was initially meant to pay your mortgage or to purchase presents for a loved one. You might feel like your entire world is falling apart and that you have no control over this gambling.

When negative emotions overwhelm you, just stop and breathe.

Inhale and exhale deeply. Center yourself and remember that no situation is so bad that it cannot be fixed. **No situation is so bad that you have to harm yourself.**

Make a choice to align your thoughts to positivity and also productivity. You do not need a New Year or even a new day to start. You can choose right now, in this moment, to cast off all negativity and to think better, healthier thoughts.

Naturally, there will be moments when you spiral downwards.

You might remember all of your losses, debts and broken relationships. You might even be inclined to think and speak of yourself in a derogatory manner. When these moments pop up, just acknowledge them for what they are. These negative thoughts remind you of what has happened but they do not control the possibilities of your future.

The fact is, you will have money again. Through proper planning and financial management, your debts can be cleared. Your broken relationships can be mended and you can also create new bonds with new people.

Lean on the Gamblers Anonymous groups for support during difficult times. In the early stages of your recovery, it might feel uncomfortable reaching out for help from these groups. Your thoughts might be racing, you might even be irritable and lack the patience to listen.

You might want to be the center of attention and get the answers you need quickly and it could be frustrating having to hear other people cry about their struggles. It takes empathy to listen to other people's stories and connect it with your own but empathy is something that a lot of problem gamblers lack. We are accustomed to being manipulative, secretive and untruthful, so being compassionate and supportive may prove to be a challenge.

The Gamblers Anonymous groups have been around for many years. Trust that they've seen and heard it all and know what to expect from new members. Their program may not be everyone's cup of tea but you can take what you need and make it work for you.

It is wise to follow the advice of people who have first hand experience with what you're going through. The Gamblers Anonymous group members have been where you are and there is a strong commitment to recovery and an earnest dedication towards helping others. This is your tribe. This is where you can find a Sponsor and genuine support during difficult times. The program is free of charge and meetings are easily accessible. A quick search online can show you in-person and virtual meetings that are available at your convenience.

You are not destined to be a loser. You are not chained to failure.
As long as you have breath in you, there are opportunities for change, growth and freedom.

Support is available.
Get out of your own way, reach out and accept the help.

Write about the emotions you feel on a daily basis. How do you plan to deal with negative emotions moving forward?

_____

_____

_____

_____

_____

_____

_____

_____

_____

_____

_____

_____

_____

_____

_____

_____

_____

_____

_____

_____

_____

_____

_____

WITHDRAWAL

Withdrawal is the dark hallway you have to walk through in order to reach the door of recovery. If you turn back because it's difficult or scary, you will only prolong your healing.

Withdrawal symptoms could begin around this time and continue for a few weeks. You are likely to experience many of the withdrawal symptoms that drug addicts do, including cold sweats, headaches, body shakes and nausea.

I had trouble falling asleep and then staying asleep. Whenever I was able to get some rest I dreamed that I was in the casino. The ball would always land on my number and I would awake from my dreams convinced that I could win in real life if I played.

I was irritable and short tempered. I grieved the game and grieved my imagined wins. In the middle of the night I felt a burst of energy that caused me to pace back and forth in my bedroom. During the day I was lethargic and could barely stand. I missed my friends at the casino and experienced a deep sadness where I thought that I could never be happy again.

I kept to myself and didn't reach out to anybody for help. I assumed that no one would be compassionate or care about my suffering. I thought no one would understand how abstaining from gambling caused me mental and physical pain.

The 3rd, 4th and 5th day of withdrawal can be the most challenging. This is where you just have to go through the motions. Surrender to it. Cry. Vent. Pace. Shake. Sleep ...but remind yourself that it will pass. Because it will pass.

Surrender to what you are going through without consuming alcohol or sleeping pills. Eat the foods you love and drink lots of water. Exercise if you get a burst of energy. Take a hot bath or visit a sauna for a good sweat. When the urge to gamble is strong, take a cold shower.

Reach out to a loved one for support and let them know that you are in crisis. Ask them to read up on withdrawal, so that they know what to expect. Keep reminding yourself that all of what you're feeling is normal. In a few days you will level out and be okay.

Have you experienced withdrawal symptoms?
Write about your experiences and thoughts during this period.

_____

_____

_____

_____

_____

_____

_____

_____

_____

_____

_____

_____

_____

_____

_____

_____

_____

_____

_____

_____

_____

_____

_____

Create A Gratitude List

Negative things can become so overwhelming that we forget to acknowledge the blessings that we have in our lives. Take a moment to reflect on all the good that surrounds you, then compile them into a Gratitude list in the space below.

_____

_____

_____

_____

_____

_____

_____

_____

_____

_____

_____

_____

_____

_____

_____

_____

_____

_____

Day 7

AFFIRMATION

My messes are fixable.

My urge to gamble is:

0	1	2	3	4	5	6	7	8	9	10
none										high

I am feeling...

_____

_____

_____

_____

_____

_____

_____

_____

_____

_____

_____

_____

_____

_____

_____

_____

_____

_____

_____

_____

_____

_____

_____

_____

_____

WHY DO YOU GAMBLE?

Father had a green thumb. Everything he planted would grow and flourish to its maximum potential. One time he sowed some pumpkin seeds and ended up with a harvest of 3,000+ which we struggled to get off our hands. He often sowed seeds without considering the space that the plants would take up and the consequences of having them in the wrong spot.

He once planted a Moringa tree which grew to a height of 30ft. It is believed that the tree has medicinal purposes so he planted it with that in mind. The tree however, was too close to the fence and just too big for its location. If it fell, it had the potential to damage four houses.

Father decided to kill the Moringa tree and went about this task by barking it. He took a machete and trimmed away pieces of bark from around the trunk of the tree, hoping to starve the tree of nutrients until it dried up and died.

Another option would have been to chop down the tree altogether but he said that the size of the trunk would make the job too difficult. Also, the tree could potentially grow back since its roots were still in the ground.

The third option to get rid of the tree would have been to dig it up completely from the roots but Father said that it would be a lot of hard work. He opted for barking the tree as it seemed to be the easiest option. It took 3 years for the Moringa tree to die and was a constant source of frustration for my parents.

Gambling disorder is much like this Moringa tree. You can try to kill it by barking it and going to group meetings. The process can work but it will take time. Most people who choose group counseling stay in that setting for years, with many of them struggling to achieve a clean 90 day streak. In those meetings, participants share their stories, pains and successes and they provide encouragement so that you know you're not alone in your struggles. Here you can get a Sponsor who will hold you accountable for your recovery and will help you through moments of vulnerability.

The other option is to quit cold turkey on your own. This is the equivalent of chopping the tree at its trunk. You can Self Exclude and ask the casinos to ban you. This puts work on other people to ensure that you stay away but it doesn't remove the desire to play from within you. A clever gambler will find ways around this to satisfy the urge.

You might even install Gamban software to your devices to block you from accessing gambling sites but again, this will not erase your desire to play.

To kill the gambling disorder tree you have to snuff it out from its roots. **The goal should not be "to quit", but rather, to get to the root of what makes you gamble and heal that**.

Every day on my way home from work I had to pass 7 casino-type establishments. A few of them were upscale with a business-class customer base where you could be served unlimited premium alcohol, jumbo shrimp and steak at no cost. Others were so raggedy that customers could enter wearing flip-flops and would have to suffice with a hot dog and one beer served hourly. I loved both environments equally.

Passing 7 casinos was not an easy task. It felt like each one was taunting me more than the last, breaking down my resistance little by little until I'd say to myself, "What's one little bet?"

I would often go to the casino around 5pm, telling myself that I was only going to see what numbers the electronic roulette table played. Most days I'd end up staying until they closed at midnight. On Saturday mornings I was usually the first person in the casino when they opened at 10am.

I spent Christmas night in a 24hr casino believing that I was around my "true family"… and genuinely felt that way.

In that casino everyone knew my name and we all had the love of roulette in common. There was a lot of laughter and camaraderie. We would shout numbers that we believed would play and if a player was short on cash we would throw money across the table without hesitation, just to keep the player in the game and to keep the vibe alive. Win, lose or draw, it didn't matter to me. I was free to be myself, in that judgment-free space, around like-minded people.

I loved the feeling of picking the right number on the roulette. It never mattered how much I won it for. I just loved being right. I understood the machine and saw patterns in the programming that the average player couldn't see. I felt a connection with the machine and truly believed that I could will a number to play. A loss was viewed as just an opportunity for me to refocus and try again.

The casino was an escape from my real life where I felt unloved and unimportant. Father was abusive and I grew up resenting him, then got into a relationship where my partner physically and verbally abused me. I held my traumas close and struggled to move beyond my past. The roulette accepted me as I was and provided an instant happiness that I couldn't find outside the walls of the casino.

If you search yourself honestly and thoroughly you will find the real reasons why you gamble. These are the roots that need to be pulled out in order for you to heal. People who do not understand your gambling disorder might consider your roots to be excuses. They might not want to hear your truth. Do not allow your Recovery to be dependent on what other people think and feel. Pursue recovery for your own good.

Confess

Write in detail about your gambling. Write about your urges, wins, losses and regrets. Express yourself freely without holding back.

This information is for you alone to read and reflect upon. It isn't meant to be shared with anyone else. It is the way to see the full magnitude of your situation and to take proper stock of the financial, mental and emotional losses. It is an opportunity for you to be honest and to cleanse yourself of your secrets.

_____

_____

_____

_____

_____

_____

_____

_____

_____

_____

_____

_____

_____

_____

_____

_____

Day 8

AFFIRMATION

I am doing the best I can in this moment.

Difficult moments will pass away.
Peace will come.

My urge to gamble is:

0	1	2	3	4	5	6	7	8	9	10

none   high

I am feeling...

_____

_____

_____

_____

_____

_____

_____

_____

_____

_____

_____

_____

_____

_____

_____

_____

_____

_____

_____

_____

_____

_____

ROOT - ESCAPISM

"Escapism is mental diversion from unpleasant or boring aspects of daily life, typically through activities involving imagination or entertainment. Escapism may be used to occupy one's self away from persistent feelings of depression or general sadness." – Wikipedia.

As kids we can't wait to grow up and have our own house, buy fancy cars and make our own money. We yearn for independence from our parents and hope to find a soulmate who we can share the rest of our life with. These dreams die slow deaths when we branch out on our own and realize how heavy the weight of adulthood truly is.

We stay in miserable jobs just for the paycheck because a steady income keeps a roof over our head and food on the table. We never experience fairytale romances but instead end up with partners who cheat or nag us to death the minute we step into the house. Debt looms over us like a dark cloud and creditors pursue us like hound dogs. We look around and see other people living their best life and wonder why ours has to suck so much.

Most people look forward to the weekend where we can numb the pains of adulthood with some form of entertainment. While a lot of people enjoy the movies and restaurants, others go to the bars and clubs. Some escape their realities with drugs and alcohol while others find comfort in gambling. The harder life gets, the more we want to run away from it. When we don't have the answers or resources to make life better, we try to bury our head in something that could distract us and provide joy, even if it is short-lived. This is the way we cope.

GAMBLING TO ESCAPE BOREDOM

There is a void in your life. A feeling of emptiness ... and a frustration with this emptiness. You find it challenging to focus because you are unsatisfied and uninterested in the activities that you have to do on a regular basis. Your life feels uneventful and mundane.

The bright colors, flashing lights and up-tempo sounds of the games provide an escape and make you feel alive. They spark excitement into your dull day.

- Keep record of the days, times, places and activities that you are doing when you experience boredom and feel the urge to gamble.

  These records will help you to identify triggers so that you can treat with your boredom in a proactive way.

- Participate in activities that keep you mentally stimulated. You might find comfort in doing puzzles, crosswords, sudoku and mazes.

  If doing these provide no challenge for you, then create them. It could be that you are meant to be the Creator instead of the consumer. Create something interesting and put it up for sale.

Search yourself. *What is your life's purpose? What are you most passionate about? What do you want your legacy to be?* Set a goal for yourself and aim to complete it.

- Go outside and connect with nature.
  Participate in physical activities that make you sweat and get your heart pumping. Learn to swim. Invest in some good shoes and take a run. Hit a ball. Go for a hike. Breathe fresh air.

- Do more activities with your loved ones.
  If your family is busy or you do not have a good relationship with them, then connect with your friends. Join groups with people who are your own age and keep busy in activities that do not involve wagering money.

Create a bigger, bolder life. Make a conscious effort to experience new places, cultures and foods. Get off your devices and delve into the diversity of the world.

GAMBLING TO ESCAPE STRESS

My partner of 10 years walked out on me the day after our newborn was diagnosed with a hole in her heart. Unable to work because of our child's hospitalization, I lived off my savings, then maxed out my credit card. The bank hounded me for about a year and then turned my account over to a debt collector who threatened legal action. I sold every valuable thing that I had, slept on a 2-inch piece of foam on the floor of my apartment and got on social welfare as my last resort.

It took about 4 years to rebuild my life financially but no matter how much success I had in business, I couldn't move beyond the traumas I experienced. The only time I could forget about my pain was when I was sitting in front of the roulette machine.

Whenever I visited my favorite casino, I would be greeted and treated like I mattered. If someone was sitting in my favorite seat, they would immediately get up and relocate themselves. I would be served vodka mixed with coca cola in a tall glass of ice, just the way I liked it, without even having to ask. The casino attendants would stand at my side, tell me the hot numbers on the roulette machine and would show a genuine interest in my day. In the time that I was at the casino I was allowed to be free from my reality. I was allowed to laugh, unwind and be light.

Most of us deal with stress in a reactive way.
We try to distance ourselves physically and psychologically from our problems and run towards activities that give us instant joy.

The games give us an illusion of freedom.

The minute we leave the casino or log off, reality jumps right back on our shoulders, with the added weight of wasted time and money.

Problems can only be fixed if they are dealt with head-on.

If you are committed to improving your life then you must participate in activities that are healthy and solution-focused.

- There is no shame in seeking professional support for problems that you are facing. The world is becoming more accepting of therapy and displays of vulnerability.

- Meditation, yoga and journal writing are just some of the activities that people are encouraged to do, to become more mindful of their feelings and to balance themselves.

- Make use of Positive Re-appraisal techniques whereby you look for the good in challenging situations. Focus on the things that you are grateful for and consciously work on developing an optimistic spirit.

- Find the lessons in your trials. Turn your mess into a message. Strive to heal yourself so that you can turn around and help to free someone else.

The goal is to be proactive, to develop your coping skills and to embrace new ways of treating with your problems. Stay grounded in reality and not look for a way to escape the things that are unpleasant or difficult.

Do you gamble to Escape?
Write about the things that push you to escape your reality.
What steps will you take to fix these problems?

_____

_____

_____

_____

_____

_____

_____

_____

_____

_____

_____

_____

_____

_____

_____

_____

_____

_____

_____

_____

_____

_____

Engage In Volunteer Work

Devote at least an hour of your time to helping someone else. You can contact a local charitable organization and find out if they need volunteers. Be of service to a relative or a neighbor who may need some assistance. Spend some time focusing on service to others.

Day 9

AFFIRMATION

I am not my worst sin.
Gambling does not define me.

My urge to gamble is:

0	1	2	3	4	5	6	7	8	9	10
none										high

I am feeling...

_____

_____

_____

_____

_____

_____

_____

_____

_____

_____

_____

_____

_____

_____

_____

_____

_____

_____

_____

_____

_____

_____

ROOT - IDENTITY

GAMBLING AS PART OF YOUR IDENTITY

Do you feel connected to a particular game? Do you feel a connection so deep that you believe the game is part of who you are? Do you take pride in being someone who excels at that game and cannot seem to understand why other people would play games that are inferior to it?

I've seen this especially with poker players who walk through the casino with their heads held high, turning their noses down on slot players. There is a certain esteem when one is able to master poker, to sit at tables with high buy-ins and to compete in tournaments. It evolves from being entertainment and attaches itself to part of one's identity.

I gambled at a tiny Chinese-owned casino for several years. It was a dingy, rundown establishment with poor lighting and old machines. It was a crappy place, so the odds of running into someone I knew were slim to none. The roulette machines were seldom serviced so they often malfunctioned and played the same number repeatedly. Over time, that casino expanded and became a multistorey Vegas-like establishment with marble floors and walls. They installed top of the line machines and decorated with porcelain vases and 10 foot statues of Greek goddesses. The regular gamblers often made remarks like "Look what my money built." There was almost a sense of pride and ownership and no one felt bad that these upgrades were made possible because of their losses.

There was a gentleman who gambled in the casino every day at my favorite table. While most people wore jeans and a t-shirt, he was always impeccably attired in neatly ironed shirts and dress pants. After placing his bets, he stood silently with his hands in his pants pockets and watched the roulette wheel spin, while other players shouted at it to deliver their number.

Whether he won or lost, the gentleman's demeanor remained the same. While other players roared with excitement or cursed the machine, he stayed composed and unmoved. I felt a rush placing a $10 bet but he easily laid $100 on each number he liked. I imagined that he was a wealthy businessman who gambled in this rundown hole just to be free from the judgment of his peers and to share a couple laughs with us common folks.

It was a regular day at the casino, with the usual crowd at our table. We were laughing, drinking and enjoying the game when a woman burst into the room and started shouting in our direction. She wore a simple cotton dress with rubber flip flops on her feet and charged towards the gentleman to strike him with her little handbag.

"This is what you doing with the rent money? Giving it to the gamble house while your children have nothing to eat," she said.

It felt like the world stopped in that moment. The casino went silent and everyone turned their attention towards the spectacle. She hit him over the head and shoulders while he braced to protect his face. The security ran in, grabbed her up like a tiny doll and removed her from the casino floor.

We all stood there in an awkward silence, making eye contact with each other. In that moment, the gentleman's façade was shattered and we all knew that he was using the household rent to gamble. He was suffering his family and denying his children of proper meals just so he could play the game. He created a persona of someone with large amounts of disposable income yet in reality, he was broke.

The security came back inside and asked the gentleman to attend to his wife who was outside causing a scene. He left the table and we all let out a sigh of relief. Bets were open on the roulette machine and we all shamelessly and without skipping a beat, played the number 2, which in our betting culture carried the symbol old woman / wife.

The gentleman returned shortly and proceeded to place his bet as if nothing happened. He had asked the security to evict his wife from the premises. The men at the table broke their silence on the matter and told him that he needed to leave and handle his home affairs. He tried to pacify the group but everyone insisted that he leave. The gentleman was shunned from that moment on, until he no longer felt welcome at the casino.

The outburst was a reality check that our gambling had consequences and brought real pain to those closest to us. Every time we saw him, it was an unpleasant reminder that we were hurting our families. It was easier for us to exile him than to stop our activities altogether.

Gamblers form a connection with a particular game.
We have our special seat that everyone knows is our spot. Other people rely on luck but we've played this game so many times that we've become a master of it. We operate with skill, not luck. We know the machine and can command it to do as we desire. We can will things into fruition. Losses are just slip ups. They are opportunities to regroup and get better.

These are the things we believe.

Our gambling identity, our persona, only holds true within the walls of the casino. In the real world our actions are those of degenerates. We are seen as losers who throw away our money and choose a stupid game over our family.

Outside of the casino nobody cares that we had a royal flush. They don't care that the roulette ball landed in a different pocket then bounced out and hit our number. Regular people do not care about our lucky streaks.

Regular people want normal lives, with normal partners who care about normal things.

I dated a fellow gambler because I thought that it would be easier to have a relationship with someone who shared the same passion for roulette that I had. This guy was a more seasoned gambler than myself. His minimum bet on a number was $100 and he often cashed out thousands until management politely asked him to leave.

Security at various casinos turned him away because they knew he was a sure winner. There were even a few places that owed him money because he won jackpots they didn't have enough cash in the vault to pay out.

At first, everything was fine for us. He would play next to me and help me to secure wins. Then slowly, our romance crumbled.

We took no interest in anything other than roulette. We tried to be like other couples and go to the movies or restaurants but it was hard to enjoy regular activities when they felt like an expense. At the roulette table we could have a good time, eat, drink and earn money, instead of spending it. This was our shared mindset.

This guy claimed to be employed with an offshore drilling company yet he was never on-duty. I soon found out that he was gambling for a living by visiting the casinos in our neighborhood, one after the other.

He would take his winnings from one place and lose it in the next. Win it back and lose it in another. He wore lots of gold jewelry and flashed around thousands of dollars but lived with his mother in a dilapidated wooden house that was mounted on concrete blocks. His gambling persona proved to be very different from his reality.

One day he withdrew $31,000 from his savings and lost it within half an hour by chasing the number 26 on the roulette machine. He became very defensive when I asked him about it and said I was in no position to question him. He threw all of my losses in my face and said that no man would marry a woman like me, who existed as a "casino rat." In that moment I realized everyone, including gamblers, judge you negatively for gambling.

Being a high-roller might mean something in the gaming world but in reality has no value.

- If you desire power and status then search out avenues where you can achieve them legitimately without having to wager money.

Strive to achieve your accolades in a legitimate way.
Live authentically.

Do you gamble because it is part of your identity? Write about your experience. What steps can you take to fix this problem?

_____

_____

_____

_____

_____

_____

_____

_____

_____

_____

_____

_____

_____

_____

_____

_____

_____

_____

_____

_____

_____

_____

_____

_____

Clean & Rearrange Your Living Space

Clean thoughts, clean habits and clean environments are the order of the day. Devote a few hours to cleaning and rearranging your living space. Turn on some music and get it done.

Move the furniture ⬡

Sweep / Vacuum / Mop ⬡

Check for cobwebs ⬡

Dust behind clocks and photos, hung on the wall ⬡

Change your curtains / Dust your blinds ⬡

Change your bed sheets ⬡

Throw away broken items ⬡

Set aside clothes that need to be mended ⬡

Pack away toys ⬡

Neatly arrange your shoes ⬡

Spray a beautifully scented air freshener / ⬡
Light a scented candle

Day 10

AFFIRMATION

Recovery is my win.
It brings freedom and peace.

My urge to gamble is:

0	1	2	3	4	5	6	7	8	9	10
none										high

I am feeling...

_____

_____

_____

_____

_____

_____

_____

_____

_____

_____

_____

_____

_____

_____

_____

_____

_____

_____

_____

_____

_____

ROOT - ACHIEVEMENT

GAMBLING TO FEEL LIKE A WINNER

Some of us gamble because we need achievement. We need some form of confirmation that we are a success and that we can make things happen.

Life can be challenging. You might want certain things and not know exactly how to have them become a part of your reality. You might be yearning to find love and start a family but you haven't had much success in dating. Your expenses may be in direct proportion to your earnings which makes it difficult for you to save or afford luxuries. The things that you want might be elusive and this causes you to feel like a loser. You gamble because games allow you the opportunity to win. It doesn't matter how big or small the jackpot, you participate simply for the feeling of being a winner.

Gambling trains your brain to prioritize instant gratification.

You will prefer to indulge in activities that allow you to have instant achievement and instant gains. You will feel heavy and reluctant to strive for long term goals. The effect is that you will have pleasure in the moment but achieve nothing of substance in the long run.

Think about your life right now. *What are the things you are most displeased with? What would you like to improve? What do you think is do-able within the next 90 days?*

- Create a plan for your life. Focus on things that you can do to improve your health, finances, relationships, spirituality, education and mental wellbeing.

- Set simple, realistic goals.
  Create a plan of action and commit to getting things done. Work on it every day and expect that you will have improvement in your circumstances, slowly but surely.

GAMBLING TO RECOUP LOSSES

Every single gambler has experienced this. Gambling in hopes of getting back what we've lost.

We set out with an initial amount of money that we use to test the game. A few hours pass and that initial money is gone. We put more and more money into the game, not even aiming for a profit, but instead hoping just to recover what we spent.

We indulge in entertainment because we want to feel good. We enjoy the bright lights and upbeat sounds of our favorite game but seldom give thought to the strategy that is being used against us ... And there is a lot of strategy and psychology being used to get us to lower our guard and to spend money.

Casinos pump oxygen into their rooms to keep players energetic and awake. They keep the air conditioning chilly to give the same effect. Alcohol is served freely because it eases tension and loosens inhibitions. Music is cranked up loudly so that you never get weary. It competes with the voice in your head, making it difficult for your conscience to be heard. The electronic gaming machines use sounds that vary in length and loudness to increase excitement and encourage you to play faster. There are no clocks present in the casino for you to glance at because they want you to be fully engrossed in the game for hours.

The house is designed to win. The odds are rigged in their favor.

Casinos, gaming apps and gambling websites continue to exist because business is good. They are making healthy profits because there are more people losing than there are winning.

Game designers are loyal to the companies that hire them. They go to work every day and program games with YOU in mind. Their goal is to keep you invested in the game. Not to take all of your money outright but to feed you crumbs and hope of wins, so that you continue to play even though you lose most of the time.

Games are programmed to have frequent near-misses, where you fall just a little bit short of a jackpot. These near-misses toy with your brain. Game designers know that near-misses are highly motivating and increase your commitment to the game. They know that it is hard for you to walk away when you believe that the win will come on the next round.

Casino games are often designed where you can make multiple types of wagers at the same time. Some betting options may be simple but will have a lower payout, while some are riskier and offer greater rewards. Game designers know that the average person is risk averse and will spread out their money to cover safer options as well as those which have higher payouts.

The result is that a player can win on some lines while losing on others. The winnings will often be less than the original wager. Even when you win, you don't come out ahead. These are losses disguised as wins. The lights and sounds of victory come on to make you feel good, but in the grand scope of things, you have lost.

- Think about how much money you've lost while gambling. Come up with an estimated figure and write it down. Now think about how much money you usually win and cash out on an average day. Write that figure down as well. *How many days of successful gameplay and cashing out will it take for you to recover what you've lost?*

Let's be real here. It is very difficult for you to cash out.

No matter how much money you've won, you always think that you can do better and win more.

I've been here. Most days I would win the amount of money that I set out to win within a few minutes. I would hit my target and think that it was too early to leave. I believed that the machine would reset itself and end my lucky streak if I cashed out. So, I left the money inside and kept betting until it was all gone.

I lost around $150,000 to the roulette. On an average day I might be able to walk away with around $500. Under perfect conditions it would take me 300 days of gameplay to recover what I lost. I would be dedicating almost a year of my life just trying to get back what I lost. I would be hoping for continuous good luck while investing more money into the game, losing time with my family and risking my sanity. It just didn't make sense.

Gambling is entertainment.
It is not a sustainable way to generate income.

Make peace with your losses because the money is gone.
You will never win it all back with profit. Never!
Stop digging that hole before it becomes a financial grave.
Accept that you've lost. **Accept the fact that true wealth, long-lasting wealth, does not come from playing games.**

Face Forward and Build something good for yourself.
Find a legitimate way to grow your money.

Do you gamble to feel a sense of achievement or to recoup your losses? Write about your experience.

_____

_____

_____

_____

_____

_____

_____

_____

_____

_____

_____

_____

_____

_____

_____

_____

_____

_____

_____

_____

_____

_____

_____

DEFINING SUCCESS

Success is traditionally defined in financial terms. From a very young age we are taught that a successful person is one who has money, owns a home and a nice car, and has a reputable career. But is this definition of success complete?

If someone offered you $1 million under the condition that you would have to die tomorrow, would you take the money? If you were offered $1 million under the condition that you would have to be sick or live in isolation for the rest of your life, would you take the money?

These offers would be refused because time, health and relationships are also valuable to us. We want the money, but we also want a long life where we can be healthy enough to enjoy spending the money with the people we love. We want to have it all.

Everyone's idea of success will be different. Some people aspire to have large fortunes and legacies, while others just want to live comfortably. Some people are fine with minimal socialization, while others place great importance on family life and having a strong social network.

What would it take for you to consider yourself successful? What would you need to acquire or accomplish in order to say "Yes, I've made it"? How close or far away from this version of success are you?

What does success mean to you?

_____

_____

_____

_____

_____

_____

_____

_____

_____

_____

_____

_____

_____

_____

_____

_____

_____

_____

_____

_____

_____

_____

_____

Follow A Recipe

Cheesecake

INGREDIENTS

18 graham crackers

½ cup (1 stick) unsalted butter, melted

¼ teaspoon kosher salt

1 cup, plus 4 tablespoons sugar

3 8-ounce packages cream cheese

2 cups sour cream

1 ½ teaspoons pure vanilla extract

3 large eggs, at room temperature

1 10-ounce bag frozen cherries

½ cup sugar

¼ teaspoon kosher salt

1 tablespoons cornstarch

2 tablespoons fresh lemon juice

Heat oven to 325° F. In a food processor, pulse the graham crackers until fine crumbs form. Add the butter, salt, and 2 tablespoons of the sugar and pulse to combine. Using a straight-sided dry measuring cup, press the mixture into the bottom and 2 inches up the sides of a 9-inch springform pan.

Using an electric mixer, beat the cream cheese and 1 cup of the remaining sugar on medium speed until smooth. Add 1 cup of the sour cream and 1 teaspoon of the vanilla and beat to combine. Beat in the eggs one at a time. Pour the mixture into the crust and bake until just set (the center will be slightly wobbly), 50 to 60 minutes.

In a small bowl, combine the remaining 1 cup of sour cream, 2 tablespoons of sugar, and ½ teaspoon of vanilla. Spread over the hot cheesecake, then bake until set, 3 to 5 minutes more. Let cool to room temperature in the pan, then refrigerate for at least 2 hours. Run a knife around the edge of the cheesecake before unmolding.

In a large skillet, combine the cherries, sugar, salt, and 2 tablespoons water. Cook over medium-high heat, stirring often, until the mixture begins to thicken, 4 to 6 minutes.

In a small bowl, stir together the cornstarch and 2 tablespoons water. Add to the cherries in the skillet and cook, stirring, until the mixture is thick and syrupy, 1 to 2 minutes. Stir in the lemon juice. Let cool completely. Serve with the cheesecake.

Day 11

AFFIRMATION

I am allowed to grow and evolve.

I release old habits and embrace new, healthy ones.

My urge to gamble is:

0	1	2	3	4	5	6	7	8	9	10
none										high

I am feeling...

_____

_____

_____

_____

_____

_____

_____

_____

_____

_____

_____

_____

_____

_____

_____

_____

_____

_____

_____

_____

_____

ROOT - LOVE OF THE GAME

GAMBLING BECAUSE YOU LOVE THE GAME

Gambling makes you happy. You love the game and feel a special joy when playing. If it weren't for the financial losses and devastating consequences, you could see yourself playing all the time.

Gambling is like being in an abusive relationship. You know it hurts. Everyone sees your pain and advises you to leave. You know there's no healthy future together but it's difficult to walk away. You're focused on the good in your partner and hope that they will change but they keep mistreating you and then reeling you back in when you try to quit. The connection is toxic.

Science has proven that gambling affects your brain. When you're winning and even when you're losing, your brain produces dopamine, endorphins and adrenaline. These help you to feel pleasure. They trigger positive feelings in your body and increase excitement no matter the outcome of your game.

The games themselves are designed to be short so that you won't become bored easily. This creates a situation where every minute or so your brain floods itself with hormones that make you feel happy. The longer you play, the more your brain gets accustomed to this instant rush of happiness. In the end, activities that take long to release "happy-hormones" will no longer be of interest to you.

I loved the roulette game because I saw perfection in its design. I noticed patterns in the programming and loved the way the ball would sit beautifully in the pocket I predicted. I felt a connection with particular machines in different gaming establishments and visited them loyally for years.

When I made the decision to quit casino gambling I promised myself that one day I would purchase a roulette machine and place it in a room in my house. That way I could play my favorite game and all the money I gambled could be recovered when I cleaned the machine. That promise helped my recovery to some extent because instead of gambling at casinos, I saved with the goal of purchasing my own machine.

At the same time, I was focused on healing my life and addressing the other issues that led me to gamble. When all of the roots were pulled out, I was left with just my love of the game. I had the money to finally make my purchase but by then my mindset had evolved.

Even though I loved the roulette, I didn't want my children to grow up in a home with that machine.

I didn't want to set a poor example and normalize gambling for my children the way my parents made it a part of our daily lives. I didn't want my children to carry the weight of addiction and walk the dark path that I escaped. I loved the game but I loved my children significantly more and chose their wellbeing instead.

There are many healthy games that we engage in as a family. My children's smiles are bright and any money spent on family entertainment feels worth it.

You are entitled to love whatever you love. However, you are only misleading yourself when you think that the game owes you a financial reward in return for your devotion. The fact is, when you gamble, you are purchasing very expensive entertainment. **The game is designed to profit its Owner and to strip the consumer of money, time and patience.**

How long are you going to love this thing that is designed to hurt you? How long will you choose to stay in this abusive relationship?

Gambling promotes a sedentary lifestyle. You sit indoors, facing a screen for hours and hours. Consider taking up an outdoor sport to get your heart pumping and to receive an adrenaline rush. There are many affordable, and also free, forms of entertainment that you can engage in by yourself or with your loved ones. Participating in activities with your family not only brings enjoyment to the group but it helps to strengthen bonds and repair broken relationships. Everyone benefits in a wholesome manner.

Do you gamble because you just love the game? Write about the way the game makes you feel. What other activity can you participate in to get this feeling or something close to it?

_____

_____

_____

_____

_____

_____

_____

_____

_____

_____

_____

_____

_____

_____

_____

_____

_____

_____

_____

_____

_____

_____

_____

Participate In A Family Activity

Plan a movie night with your loved ones. Pull out the board games or play some music and dance together. Build a jigsaw puzzle, cook a nice meal or call a relative and have a lengthy chat. Focus on rebuilding the bonds with your family.

Day 12

AFFIRMATION

I am loved and accepted.

My urge to gamble is:

0　1　2　3　4　5　6　7　8　9　10
none   high

I am feeling...

_____
_____
_____
_____
_____
_____
_____
_____
_____
_____
_____
_____
_____
_____
_____
_____
_____
_____
_____
_____
_____
_____

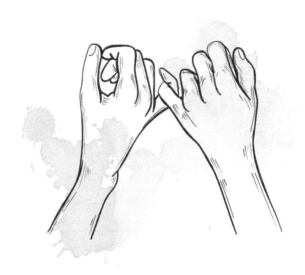

ROOT - FRIENDSHIP

GAMBLING FOR CAMARADERIE

Father was an addict and an abuser. For the majority of my childhood and adolescence, I went to bed believing that he would make good on his promise to chop me, Mother and our dog to death, before taking his own life. Each night I went to bed with a spirit of fear and prayed incessantly to the Creator for protection. I despised sunsets because they signaled his arrival at home and a difficult night. I loved the sunrise because it meant another day of life, filled with opportunity.

While the girls in my class could afford to be lighthearted and giggle about boys and makeup all day, I struggled to carry the weight of abuse. I couldn't care about long-lasting, waterproof lipstick when my Father came home at night and punched me in the face just for being around. I couldn't crush on a boy when the primary male in my life constantly threatened to take my life.

My father didn't love me, so I didn't expect anybody else to. I felt so odd and out of place that I just stopped trying to fit in. I grew up and moved through life as a loner.

While friendships are easy for some people to form, others like myself struggle to belong. It seems like everyone already has their tribe and it is difficult to be let in. I've gone to the casino many times simply to connect with people and to have a laugh. Everyone at the casinos I patronized was there to gamble. Nobody overstepped their boundaries to flirt or make anyone feel awkward. After a simple "Hello," the rich and poor among us bonded over numbers and had a good time.

A casino attendant and I formed a friendship over the years and I ended up designing the invitations for her wedding. Another gambler became a genuine friend who I trusted and employed to drive my daughter to school.

While casinos provide a rich playground for socialization, Recovery requires us to choose environments that are wholesome, to develop the interpersonal relationships that we crave.

You are never too odd or old to make new friends.
Someone, somewhere, will like you and accept you as you are. Decide that you are going to be brave and put yourself out there. Search for groups online and in your community and strive to participate in a new activity. Look within the Gamblers Anonymous groups. It is not a guarantee that you will find a forever friend but who knows, you just might.

Do you gamble because of a desire for friendship? What wholesome activities can you participate in to form healthy social connections?

_____

_____

_____

_____

_____

_____

_____

_____

_____

_____

_____

_____

_____

_____

_____

_____

_____

_____

_____

_____

_____

Get A Sponsor

If you have joined an online support group and attended a meeting, now is the right time to reach out and ask if anyone would be willing to work with you as a Sponsor. Select someone who has been gamble-free for 5+ years and has a passion for helping others with their recovery.

Day 13

AFFIRMATION

My mental health matters.

My urge to gamble is:

0	1	2	3	4	5	6	7	8	9	10
none										high

I am feeling...

_____

_____

_____

_____

_____

_____

_____

_____

_____

_____

_____

_____

_____

_____

_____

_____

_____

_____

_____

_____

_____

_____

ROOT - THE DARK SIDE OF YOU

GAMBLING BECAUSE OF A SELF-DEFEATING PERSONALITY DISORDER

We've discussed several root causes of gambling but this one, the Self-Defeating Personality Disorder is one that you should ideally explore in detail with a licensed therapist.

This disorder causes the person who experiences it to continuously engage in activities that are counter-productive. You gamble as a form of self-sabotage, repeatedly choosing to bet when you know that it will lead to disappointment, failure and mistreatment. Subconsciously, you want to lose everything because you want to punish yourself.

Rock bottom is actually your comfort zone.

You are accustomed to living in a deprived state, stretching a dollar and neglecting yourself. You have a poor sense of self worth. When you lose your money and people say hurtful things to you, it only confirms the bad things that you already say to yourself. You gamble to incite anger and rejection from people in order to feel hurt and humiliated. You are accustomed to pain and struggle, and thrive off it.

You enjoy having a secret life and find freedom in being a deviant. You are exhausted with societal rules and the obligation to be on your best behavior. Gambling allows you to remove your halo and explore your dark side without caution.

You are agitated when life is smooth, so you gamble to create chaos. You need the extreme highs and lows to avoid the monotony of life. As your tolerance to risk increases, you have to seek bigger thrills. You gamble money but are subconsciously wagering relationships, friendships and jobs.

Losses have a way of making you feel brave and even resilient. While the average person would bow out of a game after losing a mere $20, you can experience losses in the thousands and not even flinch. You almost brag about your biggest losses because it amazes people that you had that large quantity of money to begin with and that you could sustain such a hit without falling apart.

The Self-Defeating Personality Disorder was last mentioned in the Diagnostic and Statistical Manual of Mental Disorders, Third Edition (DSM-3). It was not included in the DSM-4 or DSM-5 because of its overlap with the Borderline Personality Disorder, Avoidant Personality Disorder and Dependent Personality Disorder.

Because of the severity of this disorder, it is best to seek professional treatment from a licensed psychiatrist who can devise a plan of action and treatment that is specific to your needs.

Do you identify with anything that was said in this lesson? What are your views on therapy? Would you be willing to reach out to a professional for help?

_____

_____

_____

_____

_____

_____

_____

_____

_____

_____

_____

_____

_____

_____

_____

_____

_____

_____

_____

_____

_____

Self-Care Activity

Treat yourself to something special today. Schedule a haircut, manicure or pedicure. Go for a massage or buy yourself a new article of clothing. Extend some love and kindness to yourself and know that you are worthy of good things.

Day 14

AFFIRMATION

My money will be used for good.

My urge to gamble is:

0	1	2	3	4	5	6	7	8	9	10
none										high

I am feeling...

_____

_____

_____

_____

_____

_____

_____

_____

_____

_____

_____

_____

_____

_____

_____

_____

_____

_____

_____

_____

ROOT - MONEY MINDSET

GAMBLING FOR THE MONEY

You gambled, got lucky and realized that it is an easy way to multiply your funds. You continue to play in hopes of securing another big win.

You rebrand your gambling as a side hustle and business and consider your initial wager to be capital that you are investing. You set a daily quota and play until that amount is made or until your capital runs out.

On this journey of recovery it is important to identify your money mindset. Search yourself. *How do you feel about money? Do you feel a scarcity? Are you afraid that you do not have enough to survive? Do you prefer to get money fast, even if it is by less than wholesome means? Do you desire to have a big amount of money so that you can do something grand?*

Casinos and online games turn your money into tokens and credits so that it doesn't feel like real money. It's now a chip or a shiny gold coin … not eight hours worth of labor. They want you to feel disconnected from the struggle of earning your money so that you will freely play it away. Only when you lose it all do you remember that it's real money and remember all of the important things that it could have paid for.

How many times have you refused to purchase something at a store because it was expensive, yet wasted thousands in gaming without reservation?

I once wanted a new TV but didn't want to dip into my savings to purchase one. I convinced myself that I could win the amount that I needed. In that way, it was free casino money and wouldn't cost me anything. I could have bought 3 televisions with the amount of money I lost.

I even spoke with a casino owner and convinced him to hold a promotion to generate new customers. The prize I suggested was the television I wanted. To be eligible for the prize, a person had to spend a minimum of $50 on the roulette each day for a week.

A friend of mine won the TV. She sold it to another customer shortly after she won it, in order to have money to gamble. She lost all of the money the same day.

If any of this sounds familiar, then you know that you have a warped money mindset that needs to be adjusted.

The fast and easy road does not guarantee a reward. We often spend thousands, to win crumbs. We never win enough money that could change our life for good but we wager enough money to risk losing our families and quality of life.

Consider how much money you earn per hour. When the urge to gamble pops up, think of how many hours of labor it is really costing you. Do the math.

Losing $X,XXX costs me XX hours of labor.
You will see that you are literally paying and playing with your life.

_____

_____

_____

_____

_____

_____

_____

_____

_____

_____

_____

_____

_____

_____

_____

What is your money mindset? How do you feel about money?

_____

_____

_____

_____

_____

_____

_____

_____

_____

_____

_____

_____

_____

_____

_____

_____

_____

_____

_____

_____

_____

_____

_____

_____

Make A Monetary Donation

You've wagered and lost thousands of dollars and in doing so helped to build the billion-dollar empires of casino and gambling website owners. Make a donation towards a worthy cause today and help someone who desperately needs the assistance to receive it.

Day 15

AFFIRMATION

I am capable of managing my money wisely.

My urge to gamble is:

0	1	2	3	4	5	6	7	8	9	10
none										high

I am feeling...

_____

_____

_____

_____

_____

_____

_____

_____

_____

_____

_____

_____

_____

_____

_____

_____

_____

_____

_____

_____

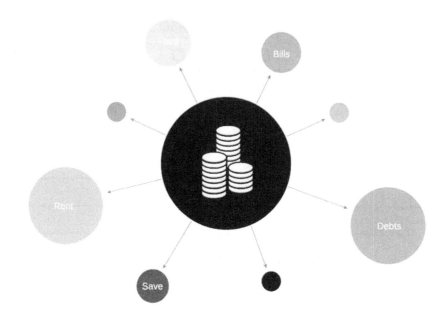

MONEY MANAGEMENT - BUDGETING

Finance occupies a prominent role at the core of our lives.

We get up each day and work because we need money. It's a bonus when we love our job and it gives us purpose, but money is the main reason why we labor.

Our primary daily focus is to obtain money because the amount we have, determines the quality of life we get to live. To have little money brings scorn and dis-ease while wealth brings adoration, power and freedom.

Money itself is neither good nor evil. It is merely a tool used to facilitate the exchange of goods and services from one person to another. Money allows us to live comfortably and enables access to experiences that fuel our joy and broadens our perspective.

Gamblers seldom think of money as a tool.

You like the *idea* of having more money but you do not crave the higher lifestyle that more money can bring. You are not focused on enjoying the money. All you really want is the win.

What important things have you done with the cash you've won? Were you able to purchase a home or car? Did you sponsor a family vacation? Did you use your jackpot to purchase a new wardrobe or treat yourself to a day at the spa? Do you actually use your winnings to improve the quality of your life? Are you ever able to cash out and be satisfied or does it all go back into the game?

We spend the majority of our lives in pursuit of money, yet do not set aside time to manage it properly. This poor money management leads to financial bondage. Budgeting is a financial management practice that allows us to see how much money we have and where it is being spent. It also allows us to reduce expenditure, facilitates the purchase of assets and positions us to be financially prepared for emergencies.

The hardest part of budgeting is the discipline to stick to it. You can crunch the numbers all day but without the effort to be loyal to that budget you will not have growth.

If you repeatedly tell yourself that you're bad at managing your money then you'll train your brain to accept being bad with money. At some point you have to do some serious adulting and take the necessary steps to create the reality you want. It starts by generating a financial plan and sticking to it no matter what.

Set aside a day and time each week for money management.

It's best to have a weekly review so that the habit is formed properly and the goals stay fresh in your mind. You can also avoid the build-up and heaviness of sorting through bills and receipts if you break them up and deal with them in small portions weekly.

Choose a time when your home is calm and quiet. Let your family members know that you will be taking an hour or two of personal time and you do not want to be unnecessarily disturbed.

Get in the habit of requesting and keeping your receipts, even if it's just for small purchases. When sorting through all of those receipts you will be surprised at how easily your money escapes you on the purchase of frivolous items.

Make a list of all your sources of income and then list your expenses so that you have an idea of the numbers you're working with. You will have expenses like clothing and eating at restaurants that you may not have an exact monthly figure for. In those instances just list the expense and give an average of how much you might spend.

Month _____

INCOME SOURCE	PAY PERIOD	AMOUNT

FIXED EXPENSES	AMOUNT	OTHER EXPENSES	AMOUNT

DEBTS	PAID	BALANCE	SAVINGS AMOUNT	TOTAL

Month _____

INCOME SOURCE	PAY PERIOD	AMOUNT

FIXED EXPENSES	AMOUNT	OTHER EXPENSES	AMOUNT

DEBTS	PAID	BALANCE	SAVINGS AMOUNT	TOTAL

Month _____

INCOME SOURCE	PAY PERIOD	AMOUNT

FIXED EXPENSES	AMOUNT	OTHER EXPENSES	AMOUNT

DEBTS	PAID	BALANCE	SAVINGS AMOUNT	TOTAL

Create your money management formula.

Budgeting can be highly effective when you allocate your finances based on percentages. For example:

- 40% - Priority Bills (Housing, Food, Transport, Utilities ...)
- 20% - Debt Repayment (Credit Cards, Loans ...)
- 20% - The Float (Self Care, Treats, Miscellaneous ...)
- 10% - Untouched Savings
- 10% - Emergency Fund

If your salary is automatically deposited into your bank account each month it would be beneficial to create a separate account for the purpose of saving. Having all of your money pooled into one account will not allow you to properly see your growth and could actually encourage unnecessary spending.

Put your money into different banks.

You can deposit millions of dollars into your bank account but only a certain amount of it will be insured. If the bank goes out of business, they are only liable to repay you up to a maximum amount of $250,000 in the United States and $85,000 in the UK.

This is the maximum payout per customer, per bank.

Even if your money is split amongst several accounts, you will only be compensated up to that amount in total.

Choose banks with the lowest maintenance and transaction fees, and spread your money into different accounts.

Notes / Ideas

JANUARY						
Su	M	Tu	W	Th	F	Sa
1	2	3	4	5	6	7
8	9	10	11	12	13	14
15	16	17	18	19	20	21
22	23	24	25	26	27	28
29	30	31				

CALENDARING

Treat your people well.

Get a calendar and highlight the birthdays of your children and spouse. Take note of anniversaries, graduations and holidays. Whatever dates are important, write it down and decide in advance how you are going to celebrate. Buy gifts at least 1-month in advance and hide them away.

Your family should not have to bear the weight of your gambling or have to suffer because of your vices. They should not be forced to sink on your ship.

Your children deserve to have cake on their birthday and toys at Christmas. They deserve to have parties and extracurricular activities and it is your responsibility as a parent to have the money to make these things possible.

Calendaring

Set aside some time to record the birthdays, anniversaries and graduation dates of the people you love. Decide how you are going to celebrate, making sure to list your gift ideas and the dates to purchase them.

Important Event _____

Date _____

Gift Idea _____

Cost $

Source of Funds _____

Date to Purchase _____

Important Event _____

Date _____

Gift Idea _____

Cost $

Source of Funds _____

Date to Purchase _____

Important Event _____

Date _____

Gift Idea _____

Cost $

Source of Funds _____

Date to Purchase _____

Important Event _____

Date _____

Gift Idea _____

Cost $

Source of Funds _____

Date to Purchase _____

Important Event _____

Date _____

Gift Idea _____

Cost $

Source of Funds _____

Date to Purchase _____

Important Event _____

Date _____

Gift Idea _____

Cost $

Source of Funds _____

Date to Purchase _____

Important Event _____

Date _____

Gift Idea _____

Cost $

Source of Funds _____

Date to Purchase _____

Important Event _____

Date _____

Gift Idea _____

Cost $

Source of Funds _____

Date to Purchase _____

Day 16

AFFIRMATION

My needs and wants are met.
I dwell in abundance.

My urge to gamble is:

0   1   2   3   4   5   6   7   8   9   10

none   high

I am feeling...

_____

_____

_____

_____

_____

_____

_____

_____

_____

_____

_____

_____

_____

_____

_____

_____

_____

_____

_____

_____

_____

_____

_____

MONEY MANAGEMENT - SAVING & INVESTING

SAVING

Priority has to be given to the retention of earnings.

Too often we do not actively focus on saving. Money sits in the bank and we consider it savings until a need arises and then we dip into it.

If you really want to grow your money, make a withdrawal before you spend a cent from your paycheck and deposit it into an untouched savings account. **Pay yourself before you pay any bill.** One day you will be too old to work and will need this money to survive.

Wealth is not about how much money you make, but rather how much of it you keep. Save with purpose. Be deliberate about it. Know exactly what you are saving for and commit to it. Do not focus on the dollar amount and think that your contributions are too small to matter. Your focus here is on working your saving muscle and developing the habit of living proactively. Focus on the percentage that you are saving and trust that it will add up. Little by little you can grow something for yourself.

INVESTING

What do you think would happen if you buried a $100 bill and watered it every day? A child who doesn't know any better might expect a money tree to sprout but a right-thinking adult will know that this cannot happen. Your money will rot in the ground and you will be left with regret when you consider all the productive things you could have done with that money if you made a better decision. This is what happens when you invest in schemes that promise to get you rich quickly.

Forex and cryptocurrency markets are volatile and carry substantial risks but they seem attractive to people who believe that they are an appropriate way to get rich fast. These people seldom think of themselves as gambling, but essentially that's what it is.

Avoid investing in things that you do not understand or things that cannot be explained simply. Avoid what seems too good to be true and what is said to be available only to a select few. Remember that the only free cheese is the one sitting in the trap. You will be punished for your greed by losing your investment while the person who swindled you out of your money profits off your gullibility.

Smart investing starts with knowledge. Seek information and advice from qualified individuals who have a proven track record of success. Consult professionals who understand the state of the economy at present and are passionate about current and relevant strategies for generating profits.

Create A Financial Plan

You would have already started drafting a budget, so today, you will be completing your financial plan. Set a reasonable goal for your savings and look into opening accounts at different financial institutions.

If you are interested in investing your money, seek out qualified professionals who can give you proper guidance on doing so. Ask as many questions as you can. Ask for references and speak to at least two of their other clients before you hand over money to anyone.

Day 17

AFFIRMATION

I will have money again.

My debts will be cleared and my
relationships will be mended.

My urge to gamble is:

0	1	2	3	4	5	6	7	8	9	10
none										high

I am feeling...

_____

_____

_____

_____

_____

_____

_____

_____

_____

_____

_____

_____

_____

_____

_____

_____

_____

_____

_____

_____

_____

_____

_____

_____

MONEY MANAGEMENT -
DEBT & EXPENSE REDUCTION

DEBT REPAYMENT

Stop borrowing money. You will never be free to experience a life of ease if you keep shackling yourself to loans.

Make a list of all the people you owe and the outstanding amounts owed to them. Pay the people closest to you first. If you've borrowed money from family and friends, settle those debts before you tackle anything else. Clearing those debts is a simple way to start mending broken relationships. As you journey to heal your life, it would be helpful to have the support of these people. Don't let money be the reason why family and friends sever ties with you.

Credit card debt is the worst form of financial bondage that you can experience. A cycle is created where you are obligated to only pay the minimum amount due and then it becomes available again for you to spend. Credit cards are useful in situations where you have no available funds but every time you swipe your card, you are chaining yourself to a system that is designed to exploit you.

The system is set up whereby a good credit history is needed to secure a mortgage or rent a space to live. Business owners are even performing credit checks before they commit to hiring, so you cannot adopt an all or nothing approach. You may not be able to control the system as a whole but you can control your spending. The onus is you to purchase wisely and repay responsibly, to ensure that the credit system works to your benefit.

As soon as you set aside your savings, withdraw money for the repayment of debts. Pay off the credit card with the highest interest rate first and then proceed with the others. Make your payments on time. If you absolutely must use your credit card, swipe sensibly. Don't destroy your credit on junk. Limit yourself to one credit card and be mindful of the interest rates and annual fees.

Put your tax refund towards the repayment of your debts. As much as possible, stick to cash transactions and do not enter into hire purchase contracts where you are liable to pay exorbitant interest fees. Save so that you can purchase the things you want without using credit. Delay your indulgences and know that it will benefit you in the long run.

EXPENSE REDUCTION

No financial plan is complete without fat trimming. Although it is not necessary to become a cheapskate, a diligent effort must be made to reduce your expenses.

Bills are the heart and soul of your budget and the place where you need to crunch numbers the most. Essential bills are the mortgage or rent, insurance, food, utilities and car payments. Your primary focus is to reduce these costs and to keep them from absorbing more than 40% percent of your income.

Telephone and data plans, WiFi, extra-curricular activities, gym memberships and hobbies are expenses that can be reduced. You can eliminate one bill by abandoning the house phone since everyone carries a cellphone nowadays. Streaming services offer a variety of programming and are a cheaper alternative to cable and satellite TV.

The internet that you are already paying for offers many free weightloss meal plans and workouts, so the gym membership can also be ditched. You can purchase quality fitness equipment and create your own workout space at home, which will save you time and money.

Source recipes online and try to prepare meals with your family instead of dining out. Imagine for a second how happy your family will be to see you evolve from a person who spends all your free time gambling, to one who is proud to be a present spouse and parent. Home cooked meals are less expensive than dining out, they are healthier and preparing them with your family helps to strengthen emotional bonds.

Take a detailed assessment of your lifestyle and pinpoint the things that you do not really need or use on a regular basis. Try to cut from this in such a way that your family still has access to their favorite pastimes, without feeling deprived.

_____

_____

_____

_____

_____

_____

_____

_____

_____

_____

_____

_____

_____

_____

_____

_____

_____

_____

_____

_____

_____

Create A Debt Repayment Plan

List all of your debts and prioritize them according to the interest rates they carry.

Explore the debt consolidation options that are available to you and see if it makes financial sense to pursue. Speak to a financial advisor at your bank for advice if you are not sure how to proceed with your debt repayment plan.

_____

_____

_____

_____

_____

_____

_____

_____

_____

_____

_____

_____

_____

_____

_____

_____

_____

Day 18

AFFIRMATION

Today is full of opportunities.

My urge to gamble is:

0	1	2	3	4	5	6	7	8	9	10
none										high

I am feeling...

_____

_____

_____

_____

_____

_____

_____

_____

_____

_____

_____

_____

_____

_____

_____

_____

_____

_____

_____

_____

_____

_____

DEVELOP A BUSINESS MINDSET

The key to financial abundance is Ownership.

Own a business. Create a product for sale or offer a service whereby you can generate income. **Be more of a Creator and less of a Consumer.**

As an employee you sell your labor, your time and essentially your life for a price that someone else says you're worth. You dedicate forty years of your skills and creativity to building someone else's wealth and legacy. You follow their rules and plans in exchange for the assumed security of a paycheck. The employer may be less qualified than you, yet he enjoys a higher quality of life because he secured some capital and started a business. As an employee, you build your entire life on the success of your employer's dreams. Do not expect security or fairness. When business is bad, he will cut staff before cutting into his own profits. If his business fails, you will be on the breadline.

No matter how saturated the market may appear to be, new companies are always going to be built. **You have the option of being a Leader or a Laborer. You can either build your own or spend your life building someone else's.**

We often see the genius in other people but not ourselves. We praise their potential but discredit our own by holding on to the false belief that we aren't good enough and that we don't have what it takes to be the leader. Life could be so much bigger, richer and fulfilling If we gave ourselves permission to try instead of shutting down our ideas. Every company that you see and patronize was once the dream of someone who dared to make it a reality. That person didn't have all the answers at first but they silenced their inner critic enough to give their dream a chance to grow.

We tend to think of businesses as faceless corporations but somebody sits at the helm. Somebody dreamed big, then woke up one day and started a bank. Somebody felt passionate about their recipes and started a restaurant, while someone else felt that they were stylish enough to start a clothing brand. They assessed what they could accomplish on their own and then partnered with others to make it a reality.

You have the money to get started. The thousands that you sink into gambling could be used to purchase assets and infrastructure that can produce a product or facilitate the delivery of a service. You also have the time that's required to grow a business. The hours and hours that you dedicate to the game can be put towards the growth of a legitimate business venture.

As a gambler, you are consuming entertainment. You will never generate enough winnings to change your life in a drastically positive way. Strive to be a Creator. Strive for Ownership. Buy tangible assets. Build a business that you can pass down to your children so that they never have to beg for opportunities at a stranger's table. Search your talents. Pick one idea. Create a plan of action, then stand prominently at the front and lead the persons who you hire to build your legacy.

Money that you generate from consistent labor is called Active Income. Your constant physical presence and effort are necessary if you want to earn it. If you cease action, you will not be paid. From a very young age we are urged to study hard so that we can get a job that pays a good salary ... an Active income.

Passive Income is generated from a business that requires minimal participation from you once it is set up. For example, if you write a book it only needs to be done one time however, the book can sell and generate a passive income for many years.

Wealthy persons have several streams of income, whereas the average individual has one or two jobs that usually generate active incomes. If you only focus on active income streams, your earning potential will be capped and you can be left physically burnt out. In such situations, when you cannot physically work, your finances will become paralyzed.

You cannot become rich from cutting expenses. You become financially free by creating multiple streams of income.

Schedule time to create a business plan. *What are the resources available to you? What are the needs of those closest to you? What services are needed in your community?* Begin with something simple that has a low startup cost. Resist the urge to take out a loan to start your business. If you have limited resources, it is best to operate where the risk is lowest by starting a service-based business. This allows you to build a clientele without investing much in stock and inventory.

There was a time when I was on welfare and could not work a regular 9-5 job because of my daughter's hospitalization. Christmas was approaching and I went to a charity event that was being held for the kids in our community, hoping to get a free gift from the Santa Claus.

I had never been to a Birthday or Christmas party so I was completely blown away when I saw how much effort the organizers put into making the children happy. There were bouncy castles, cotton candy machines, popcorn machines, clowns and face painting, among other things.

I spent the afternoon chatting with an elderly man who was making balloon animals. We talked about his business strategy and profits. The following day I scraped together $83 to place an ad in the newspaper for my balloon animal design service and taught myself how to make balloon animals by watching videos on YouTube.

My balloon animal design business allowed me to get off welfare and earn enough money to purchase a bouncy castle. This in turn paved the way for my videography and photography businesses.

FIXED MINDSET vs GROWTH MINDSET

Persons with Fixed mindsets believe that their failures occur because they lack God-given abilities. They are stubborn and hold the false belief that other people are born more inclined to succeed than them. Fixed mindset people expect to lose and therefore do not give themselves permission to try anything out of their comfort zone.

Growth mindset individuals know for a fact that their abilities can be improved through effort, good teaching and persistence. They give themselves a Yes and are open to trying new things. They believe correctly, that failures are a part of the growth process. When they fail, they are able to try again with an unbroken determination to succeed.

Identify your core beliefs.

How do you feel about trying new things? Do you enjoy learning? How do you handle failures? Do you give up easily or do you persist until you achieve your goals? Do you have a fixed mindset or a growth mindset?

Stop canceling your ideas and telling yourself that you are not capable of bringing them to fruition. You aren't a loser if you fail to accomplish something on your first try, or even on your twentieth. You only lose when you make the decision to quit for good because you believe that you don't have what it takes to succeed.

While some people get through Life in a seemingly easy way, others have to put in extra effort and flop multiple times before they see results. This is perfectly normal and okay. There is always time to learn and grow your competence. **The only limits that exist are the ones you place on yourself.**

Learning is lifelong. It does not stop once you finish high school. Even if you do not pursue qualifications beyond your high school diploma, there is always something new to discover, learn and experience. Sadly, a lot of people will not read a book or even watch a 15 minute video that has the potential to change their lives. Attention spans are getting significantly shorter and people would rather use their time being entertained instead of acquiring knowledge.

Recovery is not merely about quitting gambling. It is about the holistic treatment and expansion of the mind. Recovery is about transformation and evolution, and education has a major role in this process. If you are serious about turning your life around and becoming more of a Creator, it would be worthwhile to learn about Sales, Marketing, Public Speaking, Networking, Basic Website Design, Graphic Design, Social Media Management, Financial Management and Taxation. You have the time. Use it constructively to learn something of value.

Notes / Ideas

Learn A Skill Off YouTube

Spend some time today watching sensible and educational tutorials on YouTube. This social media platform is ripe with ideas for small businesses that you can start with little to no capital investment.

Day 19

AFFIRMATION

I forgive myself
and others who have hurt me.

I choose to heal.

My urge to gamble is:

0   1   2   3   4   5   6   7   8   9   10

none   high

I am feeling...

_____

_____

_____

_____

_____

_____

_____

_____

_____

_____

_____

_____

_____

_____

_____

_____

_____

_____

_____

_____

_____

_____

_____

_____

FORGIVENESS

On January 1st 2000, the first day of the new millennium, Father said that he never wanted to have me and that he wished I wasn't alive. Once a free-spirit who partied, gambled and smoked marijuana all day with his friends, he was forced to settle down and earn a steady income when I came along. I am the last of his 4 children and the only one he raised.

Father filled our home with physical and verbal abuse while Mother kept her head down and did what was necessary for our survival. She paid all of the bills, cleaned, washed clothes, ironed, took out the trash, carried the vehicles to be serviced and dealt with all home repairs. I learned to cook at age 11 and this became my every-day responsibility, along with painting the house every Christmas. I watched my Mother struggle for years while Father lay around doing nothing. I knew from very early on that I didn't want a husband like him.

I fell in love with a very sweet and ambitious boy who grew into a man that was identical to Father. He deserted me when our baby was 3 weeks old and sick with a hole in her heart. When he returned months later, I had already learned to cope on my own and refused to allow him back into my personal space. Realizing that he no longer had my love and respect, he resorted to physical violence to exert his dominance. I was granted a 3-year restraining order against him and resigned myself to being a single mother.

I spent 6 years alone, raising my daughter and growing my businesses. A man who I worked with on occasion, dressed himself in a 3-piece suit, visited Father and asked for his blessing to date me. Father gave his approval and said that I should give the man a chance since I was getting older and "wouldn't want to be alone forever".

Within 6 months, this man quit his job and declared that he was now going to work for me in one of my companies. He tried to gain access to my money and when I refused, he became mean-spirited towards me and my daughter.

The day I broke off communication with him, he doused me with gasoline and had me on my knees begging for my life. He held a cutlass (machete) in one hand and a purple lighter in the other and asked me to choose how I would die.

All my life I prayed to God for protection but in that moment all I could do was cry out for my Mother. I passed out and when I woke up, I was laying on the pavement in front of her house.

I stayed inside that house for 6 months, afraid to walk outside and sleep with the lights off at night. When I finally emerged, I did a lot of charity work. I organized and distributed hampers to single mothers, held toy drives, helped disadvantaged women to start businesses, taught adult literacy and became a blood donor. I was determined to help as many people as possible but I couldn't help myself.

I was high-functioning and productive at my work but a simple memory would pop up and cause me to fall apart. People who knew about my traumas often commented on my strength but I didn't feel strong. At first, all I could do was cry. Those tears dried and I felt an anger which steadily grew into rage. I despised the men who hurt me and I allowed that bitterness to fester in my mind and spirit.

Sitting with the roulette and focusing on numbers was the way I chose to cope. I knew that there were other, more effective ways to treat with my problems but I wasn't ready for that. I was in a dark place and chose to settle there for a while.

I was angry at the world and everyone in it.
I threw away an abundance of money on a game because money seemed to be the only thing that people cared about.

I felt hollow and devoid of happiness.
The dopamine and adrenaline rush from gambling was the thing that kept me going.

One day I just grew tired. Tired of being angry. Tired of regretting my past. Tired of hating the people who hurt me. They were all living happily while I was suffering myself. No amount of charity or good deeds that I performed made me feel better about my life. No amount of success in business made me happy. I was chained to my past and ruining my future because of my unwillingness to forgive, let go and move forward.

Forgiveness is a conscious decision to heal.
It is an awareness that the past cannot be changed and an acceptance of that fact. When you forgive, you make a decision to move forward without the weight of bitterness and regret. Forgiveness is not a pardon or a condoning of evil. It is simply a choice to heal from the hurt, for your own benefit.

Forgiving yourself is one of the hardest things to do, especially if you believe that you aren't worthy of forgiveness. It seems almost boldface to forgive yourself when you keep repeating the same mistakes, creating debts, lying to your loved ones and wasting so much time gambling but Forgiveness of Self is necessary. Nothing will change if you hold on to the shame and regret, and continue to punish yourself for your mistakes.

You are going to face challenges in life and because you are an imperfect human being, you are going to make mistakes along the way. Extend some grace to yourself. Be kind to yourself. Make a commitment to become a better version of yourself. Embrace what is positive and fulfilling, and allow yourself to be free. Heal.

Are you willing to forgive yourself for the poor choices that you've made? What have you been holding on to that you need to release?

_____

_____

_____

_____

_____

_____

_____

_____

_____

_____

_____

_____

_____

_____

_____

_____

_____

_____

_____

_____

_____

Balloon Release & Bonfire

Purchase a helium balloon for your Release Ceremony. Stand in an open space that is free from overhead wires and air traffic. Read the confession you wrote about your gambling life on Day 7. Make a decision to forgive yourself for the things that you did in the past.

On a piece of paper, write all the hurtful names that you have been called and list the things that hurt you. Make a decision to forgive the people who have caused you pain in your life.

Make a commitment to live proactively and productively, then tie the piece of paper to your helium balloon and release it. Release the past and all of the negativity that surrounds it. As the balloon rises into the atmosphere, visualize a new you rising out of a dark place and stepping into a bright future.

If you are unable to secure a helium balloon for this ceremony or believe that it would be hazardous for the environment then have a simple fire ceremony in your home. Tear your paper into little pieces and set it ablaze. As it burns, visualize a new and improved you rising from the ashes.

Day 20

AFFIRMATION

My good name will be restored.

My urge to gamble is:

0	1	2	3	4	5	6	7	8	9	10
none										high

I am feeling...

_____

_____

_____

_____

_____

_____

_____

_____

_____

_____

_____

_____

_____

_____

_____

_____

_____

_____

_____

_____

BUILDING A POSITIVE REPUTATION

If you donate $20,000 towards the building of a church or give it to charity, you will be praised for your generosity. If you lose $20,000 through gambling, your family will be upset. In both scenarios you will have $20,000 less in your bank account but people will respect you differently based on what you did with the money. In this example it's a case of morality. Charity is viewed as good, while gambling has a negative stigma attached to it.

If you won $20,000 you will be celebrated and possibly envied because people love and embrace winners. They despise losses because it affects their livelihood and they despise the risk you take with their quality of life. Nobody enjoys debt and lack. People want to have nice things. They crave stability and security, and money is the tool which facilitates this. When you gamble, you wager your loved one's happiness and trust. When you gamble and lose, all they see is you making their lives harder, over a game. People do not want to be attached to someone who could potentially cause them to lose everything.

Spouses want to be loved and they want to be treated as a priority. They want you to make time for the relationship and to enjoy being with them. Nobody wants to compete with a casino or gambling website for attention.

If you want to maintain good relationships with family, friends and co-workers then you have to act in ways that are socially appropriate. You have to make choices that bring happiness and growth to the group. Gambling often brings devastation and embarrassment. It will never be an appropriate choice.

I once worked for a Company run by a woman who inherited it from her father. During my tenure, I never heard her give positive feedback to employers who called to get information about former employees. No matter how dedicated a worker was to their job, she always found a reason to advise the new employer to choose someone else.

A couple of years after I left her Company, I was being considered for a job at one of the leading newspapers in my country. I remembered the way she dealt with my former co-workers so I used other employers as references. Still, I wondered what she would have said about me. I thought about it so much that eventually I gave in to my curiosity. I disguised my voice, placed the call and listened for 20 minutes as she tried to justify why I shouldn't be hired.

She said that I was a loner, had no friends and failed to participate in activities outside of working hours with staff members. She then cited the 1 instance during my 4-year tenure when I refused to work an overtime shift. Towards the end of the conversation she said that she heard I had a gambling problem. Believing that she was speaking with someone from the newspaper's HR department, she pleaded 5 times that I keep her comments a secret and not let it get back to ... me.

When I came off the phone I laughed at the foolishness of it all.
I worked for this woman for 4 years yet she couldn't recognize my voice on the phone. I spent all those years contributing to the growth of her business and without conscience, she tried to block my opportunity for career growth. To top it off, she threw in my past as a gambler to discredit me. This woman had no first-hand knowledge of my journey as a gambler, my struggles or my successes. She heard someone mention that I gambled and chose to weaponize that information. Her intention was to hurt me but she hid like a coward and begged for her words to remain a secret.

People like her, expect you to cower in shame because of your past as a gambler. They expect the world to be small-minded and pathetic like them and to treat you with scorn. But the world is bigger than your village and the people who reside there.

The finger-pointing critics will hold on to your sins and remind you of them every chance they get. Their aim is to shame and belittle you because it makes them feel morally superior. These people are not to be feared. Whatever they say to hurt you will be turned around to profit you. Sensible people will see how far you've come and they will be inspired by your journey.

Own your mistakes. Learn your lessons and heal. Speak about your experiences without fear or shame. Declare your truth and cleanse your spirit.

Put in the work to build back a good reputation. Consciously combat the negativity that your gambling has caused. Turn your mess into a message of hope so that you can help someone else through their recovery. Seize control of the narrative and do not allow anyone to use your past against you.

Engage in random acts of goodness.
Volunteer your time at a shelter, soup kitchen or other charitable organization. Plant a community garden or help to restore a communal space. Raise awareness about a problem and work towards a solution. Aim to be known as a person who does things for the improvement of your community.

Do as much good as you can to counteract the negativity of your gambling past. Let your light shine so bright that it overpowers the dark spirit of anyone who tries to bring you down to their level.

HEALING BROKEN RELATIONSHIPS

How has your gambling affected the people around you? Do your family and friends watch your every move and interrogate you about your whereabouts? Are your loved ones still trying to get you help or have they thrown in the towel and distanced themselves?

Getting out of debt is significantly easier than rebuilding broken trust. You can read several books on improving your financial life but there is no step by step manual that is proven to mend broken hearts. At this point, nobody cares what you have to say. They've heard all of the empty promises before, so your words will be met with skepticism and scorn.

Your loved ones want to see consistent, improved behavior. They don't want to hear you talk about quitting. They want to see you put in the work. They want to see you self exclude, appoint a financial guardian, get a sponsor, participate in meetings, journal, rebuild your reputation, create and stick to a budget, repay your debts and heal. They want to see growth.

Create time for your partner and focus on the little things that you can do to make them feel loved. Gestures like buying jewelry or going to expensive restaurants might come across as manipulative and insincere. Your partner wants consistency. They want you to be thoughtful and to do things without being asked.

Step Nine in the Gamblers Anonymous program speaks about making amends. While this is a positive thing to do, it should not be done out of obligation. If you have intentions of returning to the game, spare your loved ones the heartbreak and do not make them any promises. Do not waste their time saying sorry and then revert back to your old ways. Make amends when you've truly come to the end of your gambling journey and are genuinely remorseful for the pain you've caused. Do not apologize because it's on the list of things to do in your 12 step program.

Apologize because it is the right thing to do, not because you are searching for forgiveness. Do not apologize with the expectation of a pardon. People have the right to feel how they feel. They are allowed to shut you out and not respond to you in a positive manner. You are the offender and you are not in control of their healing. You have to respect their boundaries.

A person has to be open to having a conversation with you and open to receiving an apology. If your friends and family are not interested in hearing what you have to say, then you just have to be okay with that. They owe you nothing.

Put in the work and heal for your own benefit. Trust is slowly rebuilt when your loved ones see your consistent determination to be healthy and to do right. It could take years to be fully trusted again but it is possible.

The relationship I had with Mother changed after I gambled away her $17,700. She looked at me funny every time I left the house, and even though I wasn't doing anything wrong, I still felt guilty. I knew she would be suspicious and assume that I was out gambling because I violated her trust.

Over time, the relationship I had with Mother improved and her trust in me was rebuilt. She even gave me $320,000 to assist with the construction of my house. If that isn't a clear demonstration of trust rebuilt then I don't know what is.

Not one cent of that $320,000 was placed on a bet.

Who have you hurt and how have you hurt them?
In what ways can you help to heal this broken relationship?

_____

_____

_____

_____

_____

_____

_____

_____

_____

_____

_____

_____

_____

_____

_____

_____

_____

_____

_____

_____

_____

_____

_____

_____

Apologize To Someone You've Hurt

Apologize only when you are ready and when you are truly remorseful for your actions. If the person who you hurt isn't willing to hear you out, then respect their boundaries and leave them alone. Put your apology on paper and keep it in a safe place.

_____

_____

_____

_____

_____

_____

_____

_____

_____

_____

_____

_____

_____

_____

_____

_____

_____

_____

_____

_____

Day 21

AFFIRMATION

I am free!

My urge to gamble is:

0	1	2	3	4	5	6	7	8	9	10
none										high

I am feeling...

_____

_____

_____

_____

_____

_____

_____

_____

_____

_____

_____

_____

_____

_____

_____

_____

_____

_____

_____

_____

_____

_____

_____

_____

LIVING AUTHENTICALLY

There is a community center on the street where I grew up. People often get married here, Politicians hold meetings and various educational classes are held for the benefit of residents. At the side of the building lives an elderly man named Aldwin.

Aldwin gets up every morning, neatly packs away his cardboard bed and goes about his day. He collects glass bottles and turns them in to the grocery for a few dollars. He sweeps the pavement in front of businesses and earns a few more dollars. He picks fruits from public trees and sells them in front of the grocery where he was given a space to conduct his trade.

Aldwin then takes the wages he earns and purchases crack cocaine.

I watched Aldwin for a few months before plucking up enough courage to introduce myself. He spoke with authority, in standard English and not the familiar Trinidadian dialect. He was fully coherent, pleasant and sure of himself. Once a chef, he cooked and sold a corn soup that was so legendary for its deliciousness, the entire community nicknamed him "Corn Soup".

Aldwin has a family who he visits every other week for a bath and a change of clothes. He is not allowed to live at his home because of his drug problem. At our first meeting, I offered to help him get into a drug rehabilitation program.

"I am not ready," he said.

Aldwin and I have been friends for years. He calls me out loudly whenever he sees me in public and I wave back boldly. I've often noticed the confused expressions on people's faces when they see me chatting and laughing with a vagrant.

When my baby boy Cyre passed away, Aldwin offered unpretentious words of comfort. He told me to acknowledge the hurt, to cry as many times as I needed and to let go of the obligation to be strong. He said that the pain might never go away but that I would have so many more days of ups and downs, that over time, it wouldn't feel so raw ... and he was right.

Aldwin shows interest in my wellbeing, whether I gave him money or not. He encourages me and often says how proud of me he is.

When I was having my next child, he touched my growing belly and beamed like a proud grandfather. This homeless man, this vagrant, has been one of the most genuine and caring people in my life.

When Aldwin is high on drugs, he walks in the middle of the road and smashes glass bottles at his feet. He screams and curses at beings that he alone perceives. He seems tormented, but consciously chooses drugs over a clean life. I cannot help my friend because he isn't ready to receive that help.

One Saturday morning on my way to the casino I saw Aldwin in front of the grocery and he asked me for some money. I only had hundred dollar bills in my possession so I stepped into a nearby lottery booth and placed a bet in order to get some change. I gave Aldwin $40 but instead of thanking me he said, "A gambler is a loser," and walked off. Imagine that. A homeless man on crack cocaine called me a loser for gambling.

Gambling, our drug of choice, turns us into cowards. We lie to cover the large gaps of time that we spend at the casino. We lie to our friends and family so that they will lend us money. We are adults who hide, manipulate and deceive in order to preserve our secret life.

Aldwin made the choice to live authentically. He chooses drugs over everything else and accepts the consequences. His quality of life has been severely affected but he is free to live as he pleases without deceiving himself or anyone else.

Gamblers need money to play.

We need our jobs in order to generate these funds. We need to have proper hygiene and maintain a certain standard of appearance in order to gain entry into the casino. We need electricity, internet connections and electronic devices in order to gamble online. A person simply cannot whittle down to vagrancy and still expect to gamble.

But gambling takes away our money, homes, jobs and families in the long run. No matter how much we try to manage our gambling, the game takes significantly more than it rewards.

How then can we continue to choose this thing which only leads to our destruction?

Your feet will walk the path that your mind first envisions.

If gambling is always in your thoughts, then your body will eventually end up at the casino or gambling websites.

What is the vision that you have for your life?

What are your dreams, goals and desires?

What is it that you hope to accomplish?

Your vision matters.

Spend some time thinking about your way forward.

Who is the person that you hope to be a year from now?

Who is the person that you hope to be five years from now?

RELAPSING

Have you ever watched the behavior of marathon runners during a race? At the beginning they tend to huddle together in a group and run at the same pace. Nobody aims to take the lead or separate themselves from the group. Only towards the end of the race do the runners break away and speed up until someone is declared the winner.

I ran a 5K marathon some years ago and disregarded this strategy. As soon as the race began, I took off and created a huge gap away from the other runners. I competed in several 100m sprinting events before, so all I knew was to run out the starting blocks quickly and get ahead.

Halfway through the marathon I began to doubt my ability to finish. I was thirsty and exhausted, and felt my body shutting down. The gap I created began to narrow, then I watched in horror as other runners passed me by. This marathon was nothing like the 100m sprint. I finished in 39th place and with a bruised ego, vowed never to run the race again.

When the marathon was over, the winner pulled me aside and explained that it was necessary for runners to pace themselves and conserve energy, so that they could be able to finish strong. This was the way to run the race. Nothing outside of this method would guarantee success. The mindset that I had for winning the 100m event was useless here. The following year I trained, followed the appropriate strategy and placed 6th.

Recovery is much like this 5K marathon. It is a long trek, not a quick sprint. Recovery is about retraining your brain and adopting new patterns of behavior. These things do not happen overnight. You have to be okay with choosing the slow path and pacing yourself for the long journey ahead.

Relapsing is common. It is almost guaranteed to happen if you haven't put preventative measures in place, gotten to the root of why you gamble and substituted gambling for something healthier. Relapse starts with a single thought. Maybe you think that your streak of bad luck has worn off. Maybe you're curious to see if it's possible for you to play a little and walk away. Or it could be that you just miss your old habit. One thought spirals into another and the urge to play grows.

Whatever your reason is for going back to the game, just know that you're not the first gambler to experience this. Many of us have relapsed several times and because of this we can say that relapse is not the end of the world. Redemption is always possible.

When you truly want a gambling-free life, you'll do the work to secure your freedom. Nobody can rush your growth or force you to want better for yourself. **That desire for a more meaningful life has to come from within and you have to consciously transform into the kind of person you want to be.**

Recovery is not punishment. It is not boring or unfulfilling. Recovery actually brings peace and ease. It means having money, growing money in a legitimate way, having healthy relationships and building a good reputation.

I cannot tell you the last day I gambled. I never wrote it down and it is not something I care to remember. I woke up one day, made a choice to live a clean life and just moved forward. I know that counting gamble-free days is the popular and accepted thing to do in recovery. This is why I structured this workbook as a 21-Day guide but I personally don't see any value in counting gamble-free days. This is my belief and you are free to agree or disagree.

I started gambling when I was a child and continued for 20+ years. When I made the decision to quit, I wanted to be free from that life in every way. Free from betting, thinking and speaking about it. I didn't want to identify as a compulsive gambler and have to introduce myself to strangers in that way. There is so much more to who I am than being a gambler. I am a whole, beautiful, amazing person outside of this bad habit. There's no way that I was going to brand myself for life and drag my sins and shames of yesterday into my tomorrow.

Counting gamble-free days gives too much importance to something that is already dead. I believe in burying everything that has to do with gambling and just moving forward. Counting gamble-free days keeps gambling fresh and present in the mind. It keeps the mind focused on the past instead of on things that bring freedom and growth. People get so caught up in counting days that it becomes their whole personality. It's like chaining yourself to a rotting carcass and dragging it with you for the rest of your life. How can this be freedom?

Too often we buy into traditional ways of doing things. We believe that it is the right and proper way but never consider if it's actually working for our benefit. Counting gamble-free days might have value to some people but it could be detrimental to the mental wellbeing of others. When a person relapses, they have the added weight of disappointment for not making it past a certain number of days. They're back to the shame of Day 1 while other people brag about making their 90+ days. It brings an element of failure and unworthiness into something that should just be about living a healthy, balanced life.

If counting gamble-free days works for you then do it but if the practice makes you feel like a failure, then let it go. Your recovery doesn't have to look like anybody else's to be valid.

I see great value in the Gamblers Anonymous group meetings because it provides a free, safe space for people to talk, vent, receive support and heal.

I do not agree with the Organization's position on a "Higher Power". Step Two of their program calls for us to believe that a Power greater than ourself "could restore us to a normal way of thinking and living". Step Three requires us to "make a decision to turn our will and our lives over to the care of this Power". Step Seven requires us to "humbly ask God, to remove our shortcomings". Step Eleven requires us to pray and meditate to "improve our conscious contact with God" and pray "only for knowledge of His will for us".

This position of a Higher Power and the requirement to pray to God makes it seem like Recovery is exclusively available to believers only. This reliance on God to restore our lives according to His will makes it seem like we have no control over our actions and are powerless to do better on our own.

My friend, you are not weak or powerless. You made certain choices and those choices have consequences. Make better decisions and fix your life. The Devil didn't make you gamble and God isn't responsible for patching things up. You need to stop wallowing in self-pity and start doing some serious adulting. Stop looking for someone else to do the work that you are supposed to do. Look in the mirror and hold that person accountable. No amount of prayer is going to reduce your debt. Get off your knees and create a financial plan. Put preventative measures in place and find a way to grow your money legitimately.

I believe in a Creator. I believe that somebody created the universe and all that exists in it. I have explored God through the lens of Christianity, Hinduism, Buddhism and Islamic teachings. Still, I will not force my spiritual beliefs on anyone. What I know for sure is that Recovery is available to everyone regardless of their belief or disbelief in God. Recovery is available to everyone, no matter your religion or spiritual connection.

The *One Gambler To Another* 12-Step Program looks like this:-

1 - Make the decision to quit gambling.

- Make a conscious choice to stop when you realize that gambling is a complete waste of time, energy and money. Gambling is a billion-dollar industry built on the tears of losers. It is not something designed to help you achieve financial security. It is a business that sells very expensive entertainment. Every cent that you wager improves the lives of the Owners of casinos and gambling websites. Your money goes into their pockets so that they can live luxuriously while you suffer and scrunt. Every time you play, they win.

- Quit on a day when you have money in your hand. This is the day when your choice really matters.

- Accept that you will never win back what you've lost. Accept that the money is gone and move forward.

2 - **Strengthen your NO!**

- Self-Exclude if the option exists for you to do so.

- Install Gamban software if you are prone to gambling online.

- Appoint a Financial Guardian who will help to manage your money. This person will hold your debit and credit cards, and they will distribute money based on the budget you create.

- Keep very little cash on you.

- Attend and participate in online or in-person meetings. Take what you need and make it work for you.

- Get a Sponsor who will hold you accountable and will help you through difficult times.

- Avoid visiting places where games are present. Be upfront with loved ones about why you cannot socialize at certain establishments.

3 - **Choose healthy speech.**

- Consider yourself a Person In Recovery.

- Speak of yourself in favorable terms and avoid adopting the labels "compulsive gambler" and "addict".

- Speak about healing and goodness instead of your woes. Encourage yourself and choose the company of people who uplift you instead of those who constantly remind you of your destructive past.

4 - Manage negative emotions.
- Accept that you will have bad days. Give yourself time to process your emotions and hold on to the fact that better days are ahead.

- Create a list of things that you can do to improve your mood. Listen to music. Go for a run. Chat with a friend.

- Extend compassion to yourself. Treat yourself with the same level of kindness that you would to a friend who is going through a hard time. Work on loving yourself and remember that you are worthy of good things.

5 - Examine yourself and get to the root of why you gamble.
- There is something that pushes you to gamble and you need to figure out what that is. *What are you running from? What are you trying to gain?* Get to the root of your problem and take deliberate steps to fix it.

- Explore the option of professional counseling and therapy. Invest in your mental health.

6 -   Develop a healthy money mindset.

-    Think of money as a tool that's used to improve the quality of your life. Think beyond just having lots of money. Focus on the things that money will allow to become part of your reality.

-    Work towards developing an abundance mindset. A scarcity mindset leads to gambling out of desperation and will deplete your funds even further.

-    Focus on long-term goals and rewards instead of seeking instant gratification. Work on yourself to eliminate greed and gluttony.

-    When you feel the urge to gamble, make a donation to charity.

7 -   Create a financial plan.

-    Budget, save, invest and grow your money legitimately.
     Accept that long-lasting wealth cannot come from playing a game. Choose the slow road and remember that it is possible to build something meaningful and sustainable over time.

-    Record notable dates, birthdays, anniversaries and holidays and plan in advance how you intend to celebrate.

-    Get in the habit of purchasing gifts for your loved ones at least one month in advance. Purchasing items in advance and storing them away ensures that you have tokens of appreciation for your loved ones even if relapse occurs.

8 -   **Create a debt repayment and expense reduction plan.**

-     Honor your debts and diligently pay what you owe.
      Pay your loved ones first and then tackle debts with the highest
      interest rates.

-     Stop taking loans and digging a deeper financial hole for yourself.
      Strive to be a lender instead of a borrower.

-     Find ways to reduce your expenses. Cutting corners will not
      make you rich but it will help you to cut unnecessary spending.

9 -   **Create more. Consume less.**

-     Create a product for sale or start a service-based business.
      Use your money to purchase assets that could generate income.
      Work towards creating several streams of Passive income.

-     Strive to be the Leader and the Owner. Evolve from being the
      Consumer who sells their time and labor for wages and depends
      on credit to survive. Aim to create jobs. Purchase other people's
      time. Hire them to build your legacy.

-     Work towards developing a Growth mindset. There is always
      something new to learn. Invest in your education and put your
      time to good use.

10 -   Forgive yourself and others.

-       Forgiveness is when you make the conscious choice to heal and move forward without bitterness, resentment and hurt. You are allowed to be free from your mistakes, so forgive yourself and take positive steps to do better.

-       Forgive the people who hurt you. Forgiving them is not a pardon or condoning of evil but rather, it is freeing yourself from the power that they have to hurt you.

-       Let go of the past. Accept what has happened and move on. Face forward and build a better tomorrow.

11 -   Build a positive reputation.

-       If you want to have good relationships then you have to act in ways that are socially appropriate. Do things that bring goodness and ease to the people around you. Avoid behaviors that cause shame and regret.

-       Strive to be present and attentive, as you give more of your time to your family. Your loved ones will cherish moments of laughter and bonding more than the material things you give them.

-       Find ways to lift other people and improve their lives. Heal yourself so that you can be a source of light and hope to someone else during their dark days.

12 -   Live Authentically.

- Make a choice to live openly and truthfully. Strive to be a person who is genuine instead of one who lies, deceives and manipulates.

- If you are not ready to walk away from gambling at least be upfront about it with the people in your life. Allow your partner the opportunity to keep separate banking accounts and assets. Ensure that your debts remain confined to you so that your family doesn't have to bear the weight of your consequences.

What strategies are you using to prevent yourself from returning to the game?

How do you feel about Recovery?
What has your journey been like for the past 3 weeks?
What is your next step forward?

_____

_____

_____

_____

_____

_____

_____

_____

_____

_____

_____

_____

_____

_____

_____

_____

_____

_____

_____

_____

_____

_____

Reaffirm Your Commitment To Quitting

Revisit your Day 2 assignment where you listed your reasons for quitting. Read also your letter from Day 1 where you wrote what freedom means to you.

Make a commitment to yourself to live gamble-free.
You've had a clean 21 days and you have a whole life ahead of you that can be productive and fulfilling.

Apply the things that you've learned and continue to build on them. You deserve good things, so give yourself a chance.

You are worthy of redemption, forgiveness, love and a future. Now face forward and build an incredible life.

REFERENCES

1 -   Michael Stanwyck
        www.wholelifechallenge.com
        The 10 Thought Habits Of People With High Self Worth

2 -   Mike Robinson (Asst. Professor, Psychology)
        www.theconversation.com
        Designed To Deceive. How Gambling Distorts Reality And
        Hooks The Brain

3 -   Psychiatry.org
        DSM Classification of Gambling Disorder

4 -   W.A. Williams & M.N. Potenza
        Encyclopedia of Behavioural Neuroscience
        Definition of Gambling

5 -   James W. Pennebaker (Psychologist)
        Scientific American
        Does Confessing Secrets Improve Our Mental Health?

6 -   Corentin Penloup (Illustrator)
        Baton Roue comic

7 -   Freepik and the Various Artists who share their work via
        this platform
        @goodstudiominsk
        @gajus
        @visnezh
        @jcomp
        @tatoenjoy

8 -   Malte Mueller - Venting Illustration

9 -   Classic Cheesecake recipe
        www.realsimple.com

Made in the USA
Monee, IL
03 January 2023

24209056R00128